Laying the Foundations

CW01593483

Laying the Foundations

Sex and relationships education in primary schools

Anna Martinez and Vanessa Cooper

national
children's
bureau

NCB promotes the voices, interests and well-being of all children and young people across every aspect of their lives.

As an umbrella body for the children's sector in England and Northern Ireland, we provide essential information on policy, research and best practice for our members and other partners.

NCB aims to:

- challenge disadvantage in childhood
- work with children and young people to ensure they are involved in all matters that affect their lives
- promote multidisciplinary cross-agency partnerships and good practice
- influence government policy through policy development and advocacy
- undertake high quality research and work from an evidence-based perspective
- disseminate information to all those working with children and young people, and to children and young people themselves.

NCB has adopted and works within the UN Convention on the Rights of the Child.

Published by the National Children's Bureau

National Children's Bureau, 8 Wakley Street, London EC1V 7QE
Tel: 020 7843 6000
Website: www.ncb.org.uk
Registered charity number: 258825

NCB works in partnership with Children in Scotland (www.childreninscotland.org.uk) and Children in Wales (www.childreninwales.org.uk).

© National Children's Bureau 2006

ISBN 10: 1 904787 84 3
ISBN 13: 978 1 904787 84 6

British Library Cataloguing in Publication Data
A catalogue record for this book is available from the British Library

All rights reserved. No part of this publication may be reproduced, stored in a retrieval system or transmitted in any form by any person without the written permission of the publisher.

The views expressed in this book are those of the authors and not necessarily those of the National Children's Bureau.

Typeset by Saxon Graphics Ltd, Derby

Contents

Acknowledgements

This resource has been developed over a number of years with contributions from a range of projects – all of which have been funded by the Department for Education and Skills (DfES) and the Department of Health (DH). Contributions were made by: Janine Jolly, Caroline Ray, Sarah Thistle, Liz Swinden, Gill Frances and Simon Blake. It was edited by Anna Martinez and Vanessa Cooper.

We would like to thank the children in Redbridge, Bournemouth, Tower Hamlets and across England who talked with us about their sex and relationships education and helped shape this resource. Many thanks to all those who have contributed to its development: Nick Boddington, Jan Clarke, Lynwen Jones, Clare Smith, Dilys Went, Celine Andrews, Janet Sheehan, Peter Griffiths, David Lankshear, Heather White, Georgia Livingstone, Siobhann Rowland and Debbie Harris.

Background

This resource is based on the findings from a range of projects that the Sex Education Forum has undertaken over the past few years. In 1999–2000, we gathered information on sex and relationships education (SRE) practice through a mapping exercise and consultation process with primary schools in eight Local Education Authorities (LEAs). In addition, questionnaires were sent to LEA advisors, healthy schools coordinators, teenage pregnancy coordinators and health promotion specialists to ascertain the level of support available to primary schools. We also talked to children in Key Stages 1 and 2, teachers and other professionals who support SRE in primary schools.

We found that many primary schools have successfully established SRE as part of Personal Social and Health Education (PSHE) and Citizenship within a whole-school approach. What we have learnt from them has helped us to understand how good quality education on relationships and sex is key to laying the early foundations for emotional and social development as well as future work on sexual health. This resource builds on the excellent practice we have witnessed and is informed throughout by the voices of children, their teachers and a range of other adults from the wider community including parents and carers.

Introduction

Introduction

*SRE starts on day one in **every** primary school, whether the school acknowledges it or not. I can't imagine that there is a reception class in this country where the teacher isn't helping the new pupils to build their confidence and self-esteem, recognise and manage their feelings, play and work cooperatively together, and understand and treat each other with respect. This work is absolutely key to helping children develop healthy relationships both now and in the future.*

Primary school teacher

Children start to learn about relationships, gender and sexuality long before they begin primary school. As soon as they are born they begin to learn about relationships through the experience of interacting with the significant people in their lives such as parents, carers, siblings, grandparents and later on with other children and staff at toddler groups, playgroups and nurseries. Some of these experiences will be positive, some negative.

Often children will have learnt about some of the differences between girls' and boys' and men's and women's bodies through, for example, seeing themselves and other members of the family naked, seeing others in the changing room at the local swimming pool, watching babies having their nappies changed, and through images in the media. Questions such as 'Where do babies come from?' are common at the age of three to five years, and many parents will have used this opportunity to provide simple age-appropriate explanations.

Comprehensive education on sex and relationships taught as part of broader personal, social and health education (PSHE) in primary schools needs to build on children's preschool experiences and learning, not only of gender differences but also of relationships and feelings. The early years are a time of discovery – by providing a developmental programme, which starts in the Reception Year and builds as they move through the school to Year 6, teachers can help children make sense of what they see, hear and feel. Effective and early PSHE lays vital foundations for SRE in the future because it involves the development of the personal and social skills necessary for positive relationships. This includes developing empathy for others; caring and helping others; listening, taking turns and sharing. It also prepares children for the changes they will experience at puberty and gives them the confidence and skills to be able to talk to adults and ask for help.

Teachers and families must not shy away from these topics. By not talking openly and honestly they will be sending mixed messages. On the one hand, the message will be that sex and relationships are everywhere and on the other, it will be that they are not something that adults want to talk about.

This resource will enable staff to develop their SRE policy and practice. It defines SRE within a PSHE and Citizenship framework and whole-school approach, highlights the importance of SRE and outlines relevant legislation and guidance. It provides ideas which can be adapted according to the needs and values framework of each individual primary school. **It is accepted good practice to deliver the biological, social and emotional aspects of SRE together and this resource deliberately brings all these aspects into one programme.** Combining all aspects of SRE also reflects the expressed wishes of parents, carers and children. The lesson plans in Section 5 combine aspects from both the National Curriculum Science (QCA 1999a) and SRE Guidance (DfEE 2000).

1 Context

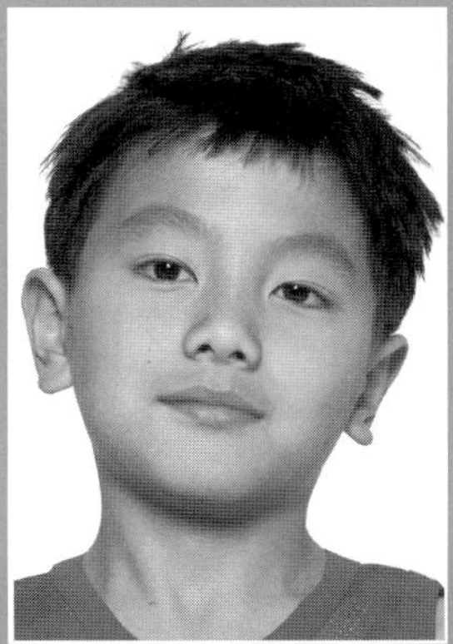

1 Context

I'm glad that someone had the idea of sex education because now I properly understand internal and external changes in our bodies. Now I can keep this information to help me cope when I get older and explain it to my children.

(Girl, Year 5)

This section puts the subject of SRE in context by looking at what it is, why it is necessary to teach it, how the school can gain from a whole-school approach and, finally, the statutory requirements and non-statutory guidance available.

What is SRE?

Sex and relationships education (SRE) in primary schools is the learning about our bodies, reproduction and puberty within the context of emotions, relationships and healthy choices. It lays the foundations for future work on sexual and reproductive health and so helps to prepare children for adulthood. It contributes to the emotional and social development of children, helps them to develop a secure sense of identity and to function well in the world (SEF 2005).

In schools, SRE is an integral element of Personal, Social and Health Education (PSHE) and Citizenship which is provided within planned programmes. It includes three elements, the:

- acquisition of accessible, relevant and age-appropriate **information**
- clarification and development of **attitudes and values** that support self-esteem and are positive to health and well-being
- development of **personal and social skills** to enable emotional development, interaction with others, active participation in society, and the making of positive healthy choices.

As well as relationships and sex includes, PSHE and Citizenship covers emotional health and well-being, drugs, healthy eating and physical activity, citizenship and safety in an integrated programme. The self-esteem, skills and emotional intelligence required to make healthy choices are common to all these areas, and it is therefore essential and good practice that the teaching and learning about sex and relationships is planned and implemented within the broader framework rather than as a stand-alone subject.

What's in a name?

My son was in Year 2 at the time. It was such a shock that they was gonna be teaching my 6-year-old son sex education. I think other parents were all the same to start with because it's the word 'sex' and 6-year-old kids – it doesn't go together does it? But when I got a chance to see the video I realised the way they were doing it was so constructive … realised it wasn't about the actual sex side of it, it was about giving the children an insight into what the future holds sort of thing.

(Parent)

Many primary schools, particularly at Key Stage 1, use different terminology to describe the sex and relationships elements of PSHE and Citizenship, such as growing up; our bodies; personal relationships education; relationships and family life; my body. Basic work areas which are covered in the primary school curriculum include: caring for each other, responsibility for health, relationships (making and losing friends), prejudice, hygiene, safety and illness. Whatever it is called, primary schools already recognise the vital role they play in building on the learning established within the home and early years settings, and in laying the foundations for more detailed SRE at Key Stage 2 and later on in secondary school.

Why it is important

Children's wishes and needs

> *Can you please tell us the emotional side of sex?*
>
> (Girl, Year 5)

Childhood is a time of discovery and learning and children frequently tell us how much they value SRE to help them make sense of their changing world. However, they also say that it is often 'too little, too late and too biological'. Children want opportunities to learn about and discuss the emotional and practical aspects of puberty and growing up, what to expect and how to cope, not simply the biological and reproductive information. It is also vital they are prepared for these changes before they begin puberty and not for it to be left until Year 6, by which time many children have already started this transition.

Children are also exposed, through the range of media, to far more information about sex and relationships than ever before. Children pick up lots of ideas and images from the media and need support to make sense of them. During our development work, many children stated that in some cases they felt that the SRE they received didn't provide an opportunity for them to have their questions answered. Primary schools play an important role in correcting misinformation and allaying fears.

Parents' expectations and need for support

> *From my point of view as a parent it opened the subject up for me. The children actually come home and ask questions and it's a lot easier for me to answer than bringing it up. I never got sex education because my parents wouldn't bring the subject up. It's them bringing it up with us that makes it a lot easier to open the conversation up.*
>
> (Parent of child of primary school age)

The vast majority of parents want their primary school-aged children to receive school-based SRE (fpa/Mori 2000, SEF 2006). Although there is a parental right to withdraw children from the non-National Curriculum elements of SRE, the numbers who do so are extremely low (Ofsted 2002) and the decision often reflects a misunderstanding of the purpose of the programme. For some, school-based SRE provides reinforcement of the messages provided at home; for others, who feel embarrassed and unsure about how to talk to their children, it can provide an opportunity to start discussions in the home.

Supports the emotional and social development of children

> *It is helpful for children my age to understand going through puberty. I think I'm more calmer now I know what my body is doing and I think my friends are calmer as well.*
>
> (Girl, Year 5)

There is growing recognition that children and young people's emotional and social development affects their ability to learn. Research suggests that effective learning takes place when people experience emotional well-being; and children who are anxious, angry or depressed will find it hard to learn (Goleman 1995). Relationships with others will of course affect an individual's emotional state, and children and young people who are having problems with relationships at home or at school are likely to be in a highly charged emotional state.

Schools therefore need to pay attention to their pupils' emotional and social development in order to enable them to learn and to achieve. The DfES have developed materials for social and emotional aspects of learning (SEAL) (2005). There is a range of core emotional and social qualities necessary for healthy emotional and social development and capacity to engage effectively with education. These include:

- empathy with others
- a positive sense of self
- understanding how emotions impact on behaviour and beliefs
- understanding rights and responsibilities
- acceptance of diversity and difference
- willingness to participate in society.

SRE within PSHE and Citizenship plays a major role in a school's capacity to help children and young people develop these qualities. It is also a key strategy for creating an inclusive school which supports all children and shows that it values all, including those with emotional and social difficulties.

Contributes to the Every Child Matters outcomes

Every Child Matters: Change for children in schools (DfES 2004c) requires that all those working with children contribute to achieving the five national outcomes. These are: being healthy, staying safe, enjoying and achieving, making a positive contribution and economic well-being.

This requirement underpins all work on relationships, sex and sexuality with children at the primary stages. Through the development of knowledge, skills and understanding in this area, children can develop the abilities and confidence to take increasing responsibility as they grow older for achieving these outcomes.

The whole-school approach

Children and young people learn from what is explicitly taught in the classroom, from their day-to-day experiences and observations around the school, and how they relate to each other. To ensure that these experiences do not undermine the messages in formal SRE, primary schools need to ensure that there are consistent messages about relationships, health, sex and sexuality.

The National Healthy Schools programme (NHSP) (Department of Health 2005) emphasises the importance of a whole-school approach, which must be embedded in all aspects of school development. These are summarised below with reference to SRE.

Leadership, management and managing change Vision, leadership and support from the senior management team are crucial in establishing a positive climate and culture within the school.

Policy development Schools should have an SRE/PSHE policy in place, which is developed in consultation with children, parents/carers, staff, governors and the community. All school policies should specifically address how the school intends to meet the needs of all children.

Curriculum planning and resourcing SRE/PSHE needs to be built into other elements of the curriculum such as literacy, ICT, science and technology, as well as having a dedicated time slot.

Teaching and learning Teachers should be familiar with, and competent to use, a range of teaching and learning techniques including active learning methods.

School culture and environment The grounds, buildings and rooms should be welcoming and secure, and this positive and friendly atmosphere should be reflected in school publications and handouts.

Giving pupils a voice Pupils should be included in all aspects of school life, such as being involved in reviewing and developing policies.

Provision of pupil support services It is vital for all children and young people in the school to be able to access support and advice services. Partnership working with local agencies will facilitate this. Supplies and disposal of sanitary products should be made easily accessible to girls.

Staff professional development, health and well-being School staff need professional development in SRE/PSHE and Citizenship and ongoing support and supervision.

Partnerships with parents, carers and local communities It is important to liaise regularly with parents and carers to establish a link between home and school and involve them in decision making.

Assessing, recording and reporting pupils' achievements Assessment is vital in order to check learning and understanding of the subject, get to know the children, to celebrate their successes and build on what's working well.

Statutory requirements and non-statutory guidance

National Curriculum

The statutory national curriculum (QCA 1999a) is underpinned by the stated belief in education as a route to the spiritual, moral, social, cultural and physical development and thus the well-being of the individual. It has two broad aims that provide an essential context within which schools develop their own curriculum.

Aim 1: The school curriculum should aim to provide opportunities for all pupils to learn and achieve.

Aim 2: The school curriculum should aim to promote the pupils' spiritual, moral, social and cultural development and prepare all pupils for the opportunities and responsibilities of life.

Framework for PSHE and Citizenship

This non-statutory framework (QCA 1999a) provides a planning tool to assist schools in meeting the central aims of the National curriculum through PSHE and Citizenship. The four strands are:

- developing confidence and responsibility and making the most of their abilities
- preparing to play an active role as citizens
- developing a healthy, safer lifestyle
- developing good relationships and respecting the differences between people.

1996 Education Act

This Act consolidated all previous legislation on the teaching about sex and relationships. It can be summarised as follows.

- The biological elements of SRE, including puberty and reproduction as set out in the National Curriculum Science Order, are mandatory for all pupils.
- All schools must provide an up-to-date policy that describes the content and organisation of any SRE provided outside the National Curriculum Science Order. It is the school governors' responsibility to ensure that the policy is developed and made available to parents for inspection.
- Primary schools should have a policy statement that describes the SRE provided, or that gives a statement of the decision not to provide SRE other than that provided in the National Curriculum Science Order.
- Secondary schools are required to provide an SRE programme which includes (as a minimum) information about sexually transmitted infections and HIV/AIDS.

Sex and Relationship Education Guidance 2000

In 2000, the DfES (then DfEE) developed the SRE Guidance which is supported in legislation by the Learning and Skills Act 2000. It aims to support schools in developing SRE, and school governors are required to take regard of this guidance. The guidance strongly recommends that all primary schools provide SRE, and that:

all children … need to know about puberty before they experience the onset of physical changes. In the early primary school years, education about relationships needs to focus upon friendships, bullying and the building of self-esteem.

SRE in primary schools should ensure that all pupils:

- develop confidence in talking, listening and thinking about feelings and relationships
- are able to name parts of the body and describe how their bodies work
- can protect themselves, ask for help and support, and are prepared for puberty.

In addition the guidance states the following.

- Young people must learn about the nature of marriage and its importance for family life and the bringing up of children.
- Young people should be protected from teaching and materials which are inappropriate, having regard to the age and the religious and cultural background of the pupils concerned.
- Parents have the right to withdraw their children from the non-statutory elements of SRE.
- Both mainstream schools and special schools have a duty to ensure that children with special educational needs and learning difficulties are properly included in SRE.

Other legislation

Sexual Offences Act 2003

The Sexual Offences Act aims to clarify what constitutes a crime of a sexual nature against children, young people and adults. The Act does not limit children's entitlement to SRE. Staff giving information or advice with the purpose of protecting a child from pregnancy, STIs, protecting their physical safety or promoting their well-being, will not be guilty of an offence.

National initiatives

There are currently a variety of national initiatives designed to support primary schools in delivering good quality SRE.

National PSHE Teaching Association

In May 2006, government accounced their commitment to support the establishment of PSHE Subject Association, including membership details please visit the website www.pshe-association.org.uk

Continued professional development: the PSHE Certification Programme

Developed in response to the Social Exclusion Unit's report on teenage pregnancy (1999), a pilot programme was run in 2001–2 to raise the profile and improve the effectiveness of SRE within the context of good PSHE in schools.

All LEAs are now involved and over 2,000 teachers are taking part. Teachers across all four Key Stages collect evidence of their achievements in a professional development record, which is then submitted to a national assessor for scrutiny and recommendation for certification. This pack will help primary teachers carry out activities that will provide evidence for the portfolios. A similar scheme has also been developed for community nurses.

PSHE in Practice *DVD and pack*

PSHE in Practice (DfES and Home Office 2004) comprises two resource books, each accompanied by a DVD. One focuses on primary schools, the other on secondary schools. The packs are designed to promote good practice in PSHE, and are written to support teachers in developing their practice in PSHE, or as part of a continued professional development (CPD) scheme. They focus on teaching and learning methodology.

Each DVD shows scenes from a series of PSHE lessons filmed in various schools. The lessons form 'case studies' which are discussed by a panel of teachers and advisors on screen. The discussion centres around teaching and learning techniques used in PSHE, and how they can be successfully applied to the classroom situation.

The accompanying resource books complement the content of the DVDs and contain further, detailed information on techniques and methods used in active learning, as well as further discussion about the video episodes.

QCA end of Key Stage statement and exemplar units of work

The QCA have developed teaching and learning materials and assessment guidance for PSHE. These materials were produced following requests from teachers for guidance on how to assess PSHE, and deliver some aspects of the non-statutory framework. For more information go to www.qca.org.uk/pshe.

The materials consist of:

- **statements** – non-statutory end of Key Stage statements outlining what pupils may be expected to achieve at the end of each key stage; these are based on the non-statutory framework for PSHE and support progression through the Key Stages
- **guidance** – on how to assess, record and report achievement in PSHE
- **units of work** – containing suggested teaching activities covering the PSHE topics of healthy lifestyles, sex and relationship education (SRE) and financial capability; which include a teacher's handbook with guidance on how to both deliver and teach the units, and a more general PSHE scheme of work
- **examples** – of pupils' work at Key Stages 1–3, with commentary and information about assessment and reporting of PSHE (available on the PSHE pages of the National Curriculum in Action www.nc.uk.net).

The Social and Emotional Aspects of Learning (SEAL)

SEAL offers a whole-curriculum framework for teaching social, emotional and behavioural skills to all children and is organised into seven themes which can be covered within a school year:

- New beginnings
- Getting on and falling out
- Bullying

- Going for goals!
- Good to be me
- Relationships
- Changes

Ages and stages

Each theme is designed for a whole-school approach and includes an overview, assembly and suggested follow-up activities in all areas of the curriculum. The colour-coded resources are organised at four levels: Foundation Stage; Years 1 and 2; Years 3 and 4; and Years 5 and 6.

Each theme is accompanied by pupil reference material and photocopiable teacher reference material. The ideas are revisited yearly, so that by Year 6 a child who entered the school at Foundation Stage will have experienced each theme at the appropriate level each year.

The SEAL resource is intended to build on the effective work that many schools and settings are already doing to develop social, emotional and behavioural skills, and can be used flexibly. Some schools, for example, may choose to address social, emotional and behavioural skills through core and Foundation subjects, others through circle time or the framework of the National Healthy Schools Programme. Links to PSHE/NHSP and to other whole-school initiatives are suggested throughout the materials.

The SEAL materials are available to order or download from the DfES website http://publications.teachernet.gov.uk/

2 Policy

2 Policy

All primary schools are required to have an up-to-date policy that outlines the provision of sex and relationships education. The DfES advises that it should be developed in consultation with children, parents, carers and the school community, and that it should form part of the school's PSHE and Citizenship policy (DfEE 2000). This policy should take note of local and national health priorities and be reviewed and revised every one or two years. Once completed, it should be referred to in the school prospectus and made widely available to pupils, parents and staff via the school website and/or intranet.

Establishing needs

Involving children

> *Children and young people have many good ideas about how to improve SRE in their school, and structured opportunities to obtain their views ensures that teachers and pupils work together to review and further develop the SRE curriculum.*
>
> (NHSP assessor)

Involving children in the development of policy will ensure that it meets their needs. Consultation works best if there are small groups of children. The teacher may need additional support to help take notes, for example from the school nurse, an older child as part of active citizenship or the healthy school coordinator. Recording the discussion, asking children to produce artwork or to 'draw and write' are all useful ways for reporting back to parents and governors.

Other models for consultation include the use of school councils whose members can be interviewed or invited to devise and undertake a survey of other children's views. Surveys and questionnaires are also ways of linking this subject with other areas of the curriculum such as maths. In order to establish their needs, the following questions are useful:

- Where do you receive your information about your body, growing up, relationships and feelings?
- What would you like more information on?
- Does what is covered at the moment answer all of your questions?
- Do you feel able to ask for support and advice?
- Do you feel confident talking about feelings and emotions?
- What do you think about the way in which these subjects are taught?

Consulting with parents and carers

> *If you have worked in a genuine partnership with parents – you've consulted them about the policy, made resources open to them – then they are very reassured and actually relieved. They will then support the work.*
>
> (Governor advisor)

Parents and carers should be informed of developments within the school and be involved as much as possible in the process of developing policy and practice. Many parents report that they prefer to be involved at the outset by being kept informed on progress and asked to contribute their views. Schools that have worked in partnership with parents have found that it builds their confidence in SRE and helps to allay parents' fears about the content and purpose of SRE and, as one parent reported, 'Now I know what it's [SRE's] all about I'm not worried.' This has led to increased support for the schools' work in this area.

Primary schools can do a great deal to support and involve parents in their children's sex and relationship education. Resources used in the programme can be lent to parents so they can reinforce learning at home. Curriculum evenings provide an ideal opportunity to display children's work in PSHE and Citizenship in the same way as other subjects. Teachers have found that sharing children's views of the SRE programme and their concerns about growing up, alongside demonstrations of active learning methods, provides a much more positive and helpful experience for parents and carers. (See Appendix 1 for a sample letter to parents.)

CASE STUDY 2.1 Parents Together

The headteacher of one infant school in Sheffield, embarking on reviewing the SRE element of their PSHE policy, invited Parents Together, a local group of parents trained as peer educators in SRE, to facilitate a one-and-a-half-hour session with parents. The headteacher then presented the school's thinking and progress towards reviewing the school policy. As a result, the parents, when asked to give their views to the school, felt more confident and informed in doing so, and the headteacher felt the parents were more supportive and better able to shape the policy.

Role of governors

Governors need to be confident they understand what is involved.

(Headteacher)

Responsibility for the PSHE and Citizenship policy of a school ultimately lies with the governing body. Governors are an important resource in a school; and at least one representative of the governing body should be part of the working group that develops and reviews the policy and programme. Generally, governors receive little training on SRE and PSHE, so schools should explore opportunities to include governors in whole-staff training sessions and discussions as often as is reasonably practical. The Sex Education Forum has developed a training video and accompanying pack, entitled *Developing Sex and Relationships Education in Schools: Guidance and training activities for school governors* (Frances and Power 2003).

Auditing current provision

When developing or reviewing the policy, it is important to ascertain current practice. Developing SRE is not about starting from scratch, but rather about consolidating and further strengthening existing work on friendships, family life, relationships and positive behaviour, growth and change.

The auditing tool

The auditing tool (Table 2.1) is designed to collect information on what is working well and can be built on, and what is not and can be improved. The

Table 2.1 Auditing tool for SRE/PSHE policy development and provision			
Aspects of school life	What happens at present	Response	Action to be taken
Pupil consultation	Does the school involve the children to ensure that the policy and programme meets their needs?		
Coordination	Does the school have a PSHE & Citizenship coordinator? Is this the person responsible for SRE? Is there a named governor for SRE? Is there a budget to support the development of SRE?		
Policy	Does the school have an up-to-date SRE policy? Is it part of the PSHE & Citizenship policy, in line with the DfES Guidance 2000? Does it address local and national policy initiatives? Has it been successfully implemented? Is it reviewed every one to two years?		
Related school policies	Are there other relevant policies and how are they linked? Examples are: equal opportunities, anti-bullying, positive behaviour, child protection, confidentiality. How are the policies communicated to children and parents/carers?		
Programme	How is SRE currently delivered and to which year groups? Who delivers it? What resources are used? Where else is SRE, in its broadest sense, covered? Examples are: assembly, RE, science, literacy hour. Does the programme ensure that pupils will reach the outcomes recommended by Ofsted and QCA? How does SRE address the diverse needs of children in the school? How do you know the programme meets their needs?		
Whole school	What provision is available in school for girls who are menstruating? Are there dispensers/disposal facilities? How are protocols regarding acquiring supplies/accessing disposal facilities communicated to the children? How are unexpected questions dealt with? What pastoral care is available? How is unacceptable language and behaviour challenged?		
Parents and carers	What mechanisms are in place for consulting with parents and carers? When are parents and carers invited in to school? Is there support available for parents and carers, either directly or indirectly (e.g. school nurse, leaflets) to help them talk to their children about puberty, sex and relationships? Have any parents and carers withdrawn their children from SRE? If so why? How was this dealt with? Is there alternative provision?		
INSET	What SRE training have staff received? What whole-staff INSET is provided in school? What opportunities are there for the whole staff team to meet together to discuss SRE? What about non-teaching staff – what training opportunities are there for them?		
Wider community	Are outside visitors invited into school to contribute to the school SRE programme? If yes, who are they? Is there a protocol for the use of outside visitors?		

PSHE lead within the school should complete the audit in consultation with a working group made up of a parent, a governor, the school nurse and the local healthy schools coordinator.

Policy development

> *A working party was established that included the head and deputy head, school nurse, health promotion specialist, parents, parent governor, parent/associate staff, priest. The working group discussed and developed common aims and objectives, which enabled the policy and programme to be developed. As a result, SRE is now taught throughout the school from Reception to Year 6. This is ensuring that the children can develop their ideas slowly and carefully. SRE is coordinated by the deputy head in close cooperation with a senior teacher from the infants department.*
>
> (Headteacher, Roman Catholic school)

Once the consultation and audit have been completed, the working group discuss the results and start developing an appropriate policy. The purpose of the PSHE and Citizenship policy with an SRE element is to:

- ensure that staff are aware of what the school will deliver and how it will be done
- clarify those values that underpin PSHE/SRE and which form part of the school's ethos that emphasises children's entitlement
- provide a tool to inform parents and carers of SRE/PSHE
- create a starting point for staff to receive training, support and resources
- ensure links with pastoral care.

A policy framework

The framework for PSHE with an integrated SRE policy, shown below, can be used for developing a policy within your school. It describes the basic information that should be included.

A policy framework

Introduction
Name of school
Date policy was completed
People responsible
Healthy School status
Review date

Information about ...
The school and community, values statement and ethos including equal opportunities and inclusivity statement
The policy formation process, that is, the consultation process with children and young people, parents/carers, staff and the wider community through to ratification by governors

The aims of PSHE and Citizenship (including SRE element)
Why it should be taught: the objectives of PSHE and Citizenship

The topics and themes: including SRE, emotional health and well-being, healthy eating, exercise, drug education, safety and citizenship
How PSHE and Citizenship supports the ethos of the school and what the values that underpin the programme are
How the whole-school ethos supports the provision of PSHE and Citizenship
How PSHE and Citizenship contributes to Healthy School development

Organisation and planning
Name of PSHE and Citizenship coordinator
Who teaches PSHE and Citizenship
How PSHE and Citizenship will meet the needs of all children including those with special educational needs
What the specific arrangements are for special educational needs and disabled children (timetabling, resources, staffing and revision)
Where PSHE and Citizenship is taught (e.g. how it forms part of the curriculum)
Teaching methods and approaches (differentiation, assessment and evaluation)
Criteria for resources selection
Staff professional development and support
How children's learning will be assessed, recorded and reported
How to link to, and make pupils aware of, the pastoral systems and health advisory service in school and the wider community

Specific issues
Legal aspects relating to SRE, including parental right to withdraw, National Curriculum Science, PSHE Guidance [see 'Legislation and guidance' (Section 1)]
What good practice in SRE is – integrating the biological, social and emotional elements; needs-based; and participatory
Creating a safe environment for learning and teaching, confidentiality, boundaries
Ensuring pupil participation and active citizenship, including peer education
Ensuring partnerships across school with parents and wider community, including agreements for using visitors in the classroom
How this policy will be cross-referenced to other polices and guidance
Who will receive a copy of the policy and how it will be made available
How the school will support specific needs of girls and boys, e.g. sanitary provision, providing a positive role model for boys
How the school will deal with specific issues, including challenging inappropriate comments and behaviours such as gender stereotyping and difference

Monitoring and evaluation
Who will monitor the implementation of the policy
How the work will be evaluated
When it will be next reviewed (once every one to two years is advisable)

Sex and Relationships Education (SRE) component
What aspects of SRE are taught as an integral part of the school's PSHE provision throughout the primary school, from Reception to Year 6

Statement of aims for SRE
What the aims of SRE are

Statement of values for SRE
How will SRE reflect the values of the PSHE programme and the school? How will it promote children's self-esteem and emotional well-being and help them to form and maintain worthwhile and satisfying relationships, based on respect for themselves and for others, at home, school, work and in the community?

Appendices
Guidance on specific issues related to SRE can be placed in the appendices

Specific issues

Gender

The PSHE policy will need to consider gender issues, and how the differing needs of both boys and girls will be addressed from both within and beyond the formal SRE curriculum.

Gender stereotyping begins at an early age and limits both genders. If these stereotypes go unchallenged, they can also easily result in bullying for those children who choose to step outside the 'expected gender roles': for example boys who don't like football; girls who prefer trains to dolls. How to combat these stereotypes and deal positively with difference is a key issue for children and their teachers and this should be included in the PSHE and Citizenship policy, perhaps by giving examples of how the school aims to address the issues on a day-to-day basis.

One of the aims of SRE must be to open up communication between genders and improve understanding of each other. Researchers believe that the Dutch experience, where young people are much more at ease discussing sexual matters with a member of the opposite sex, stems from childhood, where children play in mixed gender groups (Ingham and van Zessen 1998). This is much less common in the UK, where children often split into single gender friendship groups at an early age. A whole-school approach which supports children playing together and also learning from each other could do much to improve relationship skills.

Although there are common skills and knowledge that both girls and boys will need, both genders have differing needs. It is also important that school staff are sensitive to the specific transitions and critical moments in puberty and that appropriate arrangements are made for pastoral care.

Boys

> *I was scared to talk about it as it is one of those things you are ashamed to talk about with your mates. But I know it is easier to talk to them having seen the film.*
>
> (Boy, Year 6)

In general, boys receive less sex education from their families. Boys also report that formal school sex education seems to be about girls and for girls and pays little attention to their needs. This may be exacerbated as traditionally many primary teachers are female and may therefore be less likely to have a thorough understanding of the pubertal development of boys. Accurate information about the physical and emotional changes that take place at puberty is extremely important. Both boys and girls should have a basic knowledge of what happens to each gender.

Boys also need to be prepared for the specific changes they will experience through puberty. Boys report that their preparation for puberty is often limited to information on voice breaking. They would also like advice and support with regard to other aspects of puberty, such as wet dreams; growing facial hair and shaving; and reassurance about what is 'normal' in terms of development, penis size and uncontrollable erections. Many primary schools invite a father or male youth worker to join a lesson in order to support the boys and answer their questions.

Girls

> *Before the programme I was worried about getting my period, but now I realise it is all a fact of life.*
>
> (Girl, Year 6)

Many girls are not prepared for the onset of puberty despite having some awareness of periods from adverts on the TV, in shops, public toilets, overheard conversations and stories from older sisters and relatives. Adequate preparation will help them to make sense of these bits of information which might otherwise be misleading or negative. How we do this carries significant messages, both about how we value them as girls now, and about their transition into adult womanhood.

Lack of appropriate school facilities for girls coping with menstruation in primary school may also damage their sense of pride in themselves and their bodies. Primary schools need to make adequate arrangements to help girls cope with menstruation at school. This would include, for instance, providing sanitary disposal facilities in each toilet cubicle for older pupils and preparing all staff (including non-teaching staff) to deal with requests for sanitary towels in a helpful manner and without embarrassment. Extra support will be necessary for those girls who are early starters. Early negative experiences, such as unexpected bleeding, difficulties in obtaining sanitary supplies and teasing from other children, can have a damaging effect on girls' self-esteem.

Religious and cultural diversity

In a multicultural and multi-faith society, it is important that SRE responds to the range of needs and experiences of all children within the school. This should be based on consultation with the school community, not on assumptions of the views of parents. *Faith, Values and Sex and Relationships Education* (SEF 2002) addresses how we ensure that SRE is inclusive and meets the needs of all children. The Sex Education Forum firmly believes that school communities can meet the needs of all children by addressing misunderstandings about SRE, faith perspectives on sex and sexuality and faith communities' opposition to SRE, and by working together to find common ground. The underlying principles include the following:

- Children and young people have an entitlement to SRE that is relevant to them, supports their learning about different faiths and cultures, and is underpinned by values promoting equality and respect.
- Valuing diversity and anti-discriminatory practice must be an integral part of the school's ethos, reflected in all areas of the curriculum. In SRE, this involves professionals taking responsibility for consulting and involving faith communities in the development of policy and practice.
- We need to create a safe framework in which parents and carers from faith communities, and members of the wider community, understand more about SRE, are able to discuss their views and beliefs, and feel involved in the process of developing SRE.

Children with additional learning needs including physical disability

Pupils with additional learning needs have an equal right to appropriate SRE. The SRE programme may benefit from multi-agency preparation, planning and, where appropriate, delivery. The needs of the children, of teaching staff (especially learning support assistants and others working more directly to support them), and of parents and carers have to be identified and addressed. The vulnerability of children with learning difficulties makes the provision of SRE which addresses personal safety essential. The activities in Section 5 include differentiation and may need to be adapted to ensure inclusion. The learning support assistant may need to prepare for the activities prior to the lesson. Doing a follow-up to ensure understanding is equally important. There are many teaching resources available to accommodate a range of needs. A list of resources is available on www.ncb.org.uk/sef

Family diversity

In every class there will be children who experience life within any of a diverse range of 'family' units. Some children will have two parents who are married or cohabiting, others will be looked after by a local authority, live with one parent through separation or bereavement and others may live with gay parents or aunts, uncles and grandparents.

Understanding this diversity of experience is helpfully reflected and built into all work on relationships and sex to nurture empathy, understanding and pride. A focus on building core values of love, commitment, honesty, trust and respect within relationships helps children to value the richness of different relationships and develops competence in making, sustaining and, where necessary, ending relationships.

Confidentiality and child protection

Children may make personal disclosures in group settings, particularly within SRE where an atmosphere of trust is created and sensitive topics are discussed. It is important to reach agreement with the class about confidentiality before personal disclosures are made. Teachers should explain that the classroom is a public place and not somewhere to discuss very personal issues. They should, however, ensure that the children know who they can talk to if they want to discuss any concerns or worries they may have on a one-to-one basis. If a child does becomes distressed within a lesson, it may be appropriate for the learning support assistant to take them out of the classroom and contact the head of pastoral care.

Teachers and other adults working in schools must be absolutely clear about the boundaries of their legal and professional roles and responsibilities if disclosures are made (please refer to LEA guidance). A clear and explicit confidentiality policy should ensure good practice throughout the school. It is important that all the key groups – staff, pupils and parents – understand the policy, and schools need to ensure that every effort has been made to inform them of it.

Teachers and others supporting SRE, including outside visitors, cannot offer or guarantee absolute confidentiality. If a pupil directly makes a disclosure about sexual activity, exploitation or abuse, child protection procedures must be followed. Schools should make sure their policy on confidentiality is clearly related to their PSHE and Citizenship policy. It should include reference to:

- clear procedures for staff to follow
- using a working agreement in lessons
- making sure that pupils and parents or carers are aware of the school's confidentiality policy and how it works in practice
- reassuring pupils that their best interests will be maintained
- encouraging pupils to talk to their parents or carers and giving them support to do so.

All staff must ensure that they are familiar with the procedures set out in the DfES's *Safeguarding Children in Education* (2004b) and Department of Health's *What to do if you're worried a child is being abused* (2003).

3 Practice

3 Practice

This section offers guidelines to planning your SRE curriculum and draws on experience gained from a range of schools and projects. It looks at how best to group children in order to meet their needs and at the human and material resources that can assist the teacher. It then tackles how to deliver SRE, offering a range of learning methods to try and, finally, how to assess and evaluate the work and learning achieved.

Planning SRE

It is essential that the results of the consultation and audit are used to inform the planning of the SRE programme in the short, medium and long term. A programme that meets the needs of the children should be developed; and teachers should feel prepared and confident with the methods, content and resources they use to deliver SRE. Despite this, staff must also be prepared for unexpected questions and behaviour.

Opportunities for cross-curriculum work

Different schools organise their programmes in different ways and it is important that the programme reflects the needs of the school community. There are a number of ways that issues related to sex and relationships can be delivered in primary school. This can be through broad-based topics, which include other curriculum areas, such as new life/growth; ourselves; keeping healthy; and people who help us. Other opportunities include:

- discrete PSHE and Citizenship lessons
- circle time
- assembly
- the theme of the week
- playground games
- literacy hour
- 'Home' corner
- story sacks.

Groupings

Some primary schools have found it useful to plan their discrete provision so that all classes throughout the school are doing PSHE and Citizenship at the same time. This provides extended opportunities to organise different groupings depending on the focus of the lesson.

Single-gender groups

> *We want* periods *and stuff with just the girls so we can ask questions but the* relationship *bit and* babies *all together.*
>
> (Girl, Year 6)

DfES guidance highlights that SRE should be 'both culturally appropriate and inclusive of all children'. Some schools respond to this requirement by organising some SRE sessions into single-gender groupings. Some children might prefer some areas of SRE to be covered in single-gender groups and some parents may be reassured if they know that some of the more personal aspects of SRE are discussed in single-gender groups. For instance, many schools provide separate sessions for girls on the practical aspects of managing periods in school; alongside a separate session for boys based on their particular needs, such as worries about erections and shaving. Some schools have run a successful plenary-type session with a quiz, where the boys set questions on aspects of boys' development for the girls and vice versa.

Mixed-age groups

For some primary schools, particularly in rural areas, SRE is taught in mixed-age classes using differentiated learning activities. This might be in terms of outcome, 'a task for all' which individuals in the group can achieve at their own level; extension activities, to increase understanding; support on the task, such as help with reading out instructions; different resources; or grouping by ability or by mixed ability.

A shortage of staff may also be an obstacle and some schools have tackled this by making use of trained help, such as the school nurse and parents, alongside teacher-led learning.

Outside visitors

Many schools make good use of outside visitors to supplement their SRE programmes. Visitors might include a parent or carer with their baby, health promotion staff or the school nurse. It is good practice to involve children in the planning of these sessions, to decide what they would like to see covered and to prepare questions for the visitor.

It is important that the school includes reference to the use of visitors in its policies. A code of practice for the use of external agencies may include:

- clarifying the purpose and role of the outside visitor within the SRE programme
- clarifying the boundaries of their input
- ensuring outside visitors are aware of the values framework for SRE sessions, the planned curriculum and relevant school policies
- highlighting the aims and objectives of any session and identifying the learning outcomes
- planning and agreeing how they will work with the teacher, including the importance of the teacher always remaining in the room to support the visitor, and how to ensure that issues raised as a result of the session can be addressed appropriately after the visitor has left
- providing a mechanism for pupil, teacher and visitor evaluation of the session to inform future planning
- establishing lines of accountability between the outside visitor and the school and making them explicit.

Choosing resources

> *Activity packs can be useful in generating ideas and suggestions when putting together your programme, but don't be afraid to change and adapt resources to suit the needs of the children in your class.*
>
> (Primary school teacher)

When selecting resources or activities to use, check that they are consistent with the aims and objectives of your policy and are designed to encourage expression of a range of attitudes and beliefs on the issues presented. The following checklist is helpful when choosing resources.

- Has the resource been used before and if so what was the feedback?
- Is the resource appropriate in terms of the: language, images, attitudes, maturity, knowledge and understanding required?
- Does it promote positive images of diversity and an inclusive approach to SRE or is it biased and encourage stereotyping?
- Can the resource be adapted for all children within the class?
- Are the facts accurate, up-to-date and presented in a balanced and objective way?
- Are there instructions on how to use the resource? Are they clear?
- Does the resource allow you to assess and take into account the children's existing knowledge? If yes, how?
- Does it conform to legal requirements for SRE; and is there reference to how it helps users meet statutory and non-statutory learning outcomes, including those of the National Curriculum PSHE and Citizenship Framework?
- Does the resource include procedures or methods by which learning outcomes can be monitored or assessed and/or evaluated? If so, how do these procedures or methods work?
- Is there information on relevant agencies/organisations or other sources of information/support?
- Where appropriate, does the resource encourage parental/carer understanding and involvement?
- Is there any preparation/research required to use the activity?
- Is the resource well designed? Is it durable, easy to use and easy to store?
- Is the resource good value for money?
- Have parents and governors been given the opportunity to see the resource?

Experienced teachers of SRE tell us that there is no such thing as the definitive SRE resource. They suggest that each school puts together its own series of activities, which can be selected from a range of activity packs.

Involving parents as educators

> *I don't know what it is like to discuss these things with your parents but I would like to find out.*
>
> (Child, Year 6)

Many children report that they want their parents to be their main source of information about sex. For some parents this task comes naturally, for others it can be a far more daunting prospect. Primary schools have found a range of ways to support parents in their role as sex educators. These include offering them leaflets and contact details for support organisations, providing resources (such as videos) on a loan basis to use with their children, and liaising with external agencies to provide workshops for parents on talking to their children about sex and relationships.

CASE STUDY 3.1 It's OK to talk to Mum and Dad

One primary school in Cumbria runs 'Mothers and Daughters' sessions. A letter of invitation is given to all Key Stage 2 girls explaining that if their mum is not available then a grandmother, older sister or other trusted adult can come along. The school also ensures that there are female staff available so no girl is excluded if her mother cannot come.

The theme of the evening is 'growth and change'. Each group is given a folder to use and take home. Topics covered include: what we need to grow, puberty, female body parts and menstruation. All activities are interactive, such as quizzes, matching text to pictures, and discussion. People can choose to find a space to work within the hall, or can move into adjacent classrooms if they want more space and privacy.

There is a really positive feeling during the session, with meaningful interaction between mums and their daughters. Following positive feedback, the school set up a 'Dads and Lads' for Key Stage 2 boys. These sessions provide parents and carers with the opportunity to engage with their children on a subject they might otherwise find difficult to broach, and to send out the message that it is 'OK to talk to Mum and Dad' and, as one parent reported:

> The schools have started the process rolling for us parents and I think it's a great thing. It's a great tool for parents then to be able to move the subject forward.

The following tips are for anyone planning to deliver sessions for pupils and their parents and carers:

- Hold an awareness session for all staff and school governors, followed by a similar session for parents.
- Do not be discouraged if only a few parents or carers turn up. Begin the work anyway.
- Establish at the outset how much the school values the role of the parent as their child's primary health educator.
- Reassure everyone that it is okay to giggle and have fun.
- Build up gradually to the more complex issues to ensure that everyone feels safe.
- Suggest homework activities to support the continuation of dialogue at home.

Delivering SRE

For content see Section 4. For sample lesson plans see Section 5.

Creating a safe environment

The development of a working agreement with the children will help contribute to a safe environment in which to deliver SRE. This will ensure that both children and staff will understand what is expected of them, and will help reduce anxieties. An essential point is that no-one is to ask or be expected to answer a personal question. Teaching activities should aim to use distancing techniques, such as the use of role-play and puppets to avoid disclosures. The use of a 'secret' question box also allows children to ask questions anonymously.

Active learning methods

Teachers report that programmes involving active, participatory learning methods used in the context of a group are the most successful and this is supported by research. Active learning methods are extremely effective and provide the most valuable learning experiences for children, particularly those for whom English is not their first language, those with low literacy levels, and those who may usually be reluctant to take part in lessons.

They can be fun and actively engage children in their own learning process by enabling them to draw on their own experience. It supports the development of core life skills, an integral part of good quality SRE. By working collaboratively, children are encouraged to use communication skills and decision-making skills and to learn how to articulate an idea and share that idea with others. For more information see *Effective Learning Methods: Approaches to teaching about sex and relationships within PSHE and Citizenship* (Martinez 2005).

Examples of active learning methods

Circle time – a useful technique to facilitate a safe and positive environment for children to take turns (if they want to) to talk about a specific issue, such as feelings and relationships. For more information visit www.circle-time.co.uk

Rounds – an integral part of Circle time or indeed of any PSHE classroom. Often used at the end of a session as a way of getting everyone to sit together and briefly share ideas and feelings. Children are invited to complete a sentence, for example 'One thing I learned/enjoyed today was...'

Discussion – an activity where children, working in small groups, are given a question to answer before giving feedback on their discussion to the whole group. Alternatively, children work in pairs then give feedback in groups of four.

Listening exercises – where children work in pairs, with one of them listening carefully while the other speaks. They then swap roles. They can then give feedback on what they've learned to a small group or the whole class.

Mind maps – a technique sometimes referred to as brainstorming or thought showers. Here children are asked to provide words they think of in response to a subject given by the teacher. The teacher then facilitates discussion around the words provided. Asking for example: Are they positive or negative words? What would it feel like to have these words directed at you?

Case studies – a useful distancing technique. Children have the opportunity to consider the consequences of the actions of the characters in a case study, and to reflect on how things could have been done differently.

Storytelling – a way of using fiction to explore feelings and attitudes. The group can be asked, for example, how they would resolve the issues raised. Children can be asked to develop their own stories too. For some examples of suitable children's literature see Section 6.

Continuums – a way for children to hear and understand a range of views. A statement is read out by a teacher and the children are then asked to physically place themselves along a line that best reflects their opinion or view on it (OK or Not OK/agree or disagree). The teacher then facilitates discussion based on the positions taken.

Puppets – an effective resource, either home-made or commercially produced, that some schools have used with children to explore issues such as friendships, bullying and HIV.

Time lines – a useful way of looking at human development. Children mark on a line those things they could do at different stages of their lives; or they help a teacher fill in what they know about a baby's development, starting two days after its birth and working backwards along the time line. Older children may like to mark the significant times in their lives, for example the birth of a sibling, a change of schools, a friend moving away, a relative or pet dying.

Games – a variety of commercially produced games have specific outcomes in mind, such as 'ice-breakers' or those designed to develop relationship skills.

Collages/posters/drawings – a way of illustrating a theme or topic in a way that children enjoy. Collages could focus on 'What's a family?' or 'Babies' but could also include images relating to gender stereotypes. Posters could be designed by children to advertise people and agencies that can help children. Drawings could be made showing the outline of a child with labels to mark the names of body parts.

ICT – an effective resource for encouraging active participation. For example you can use a large-scale picture, mind map or time line on an interactive whiteboard. Membership of a regional broadband consortium or grid for learning will provide access to a wide range of recommended ICT resources such as pictures.

Role-play and drama – a way of allowing children to explore feelings and ideas in a practical, real-life situation. May be done in pairs, small or large groups and be teacher- or child-led. To be effective, careful management is vital with debriefing and processing to draw out the learning.

Assessment and evaluation

Feedback from QCA and Ofsted indicated that pupil achievement at the end of each key stage can be lower in PSHE than in other subjects. As a result, QCA has produced guidance that establishes a national standard to help teachers and pupils set high expectations and assess pupil progress and attainment. These can be downloaded from www.qca.org.uk/9473.html and include:

- non-statutory end-of-key-stage statements
- PSHE at Key Stages 1–4: Guidance on assessment, recording and reporting.

Assessing the learning

One of the key components of active learning methods is the processing of the learning, enabling children to reflect on what they achieved and experienced by taking part in the activity. It is really important to allow enough time at the end of the session for this, otherwise the group can go away having enjoyed the activity but not knowing what the point of the exercise was. This information can also be used to assess what has been learnt and understood and to inform the planning of future lessons. Some typical questions are:

- What was it like doing this activity today?
- What did you learn by listening to people's opinions that were different from your own?
- What skills did you learn and practise today?
- Do you think your learning today will change or influence your behaviour?

The 'secret' question box is a good way of assessing learning and allows children to post questions anonymously and so help the teacher to prepare for the next lesson.

Evaluation methods

Ofsted highlighted evaluation as an area in particular need of attention. Regular evaluation of the SRE programme by the children, parents and carers, and teachers involved is vital. Evaluation should form part of an ongoing process. Evaluation of the methods enables you to plan future work more constructively. Teaching assistants can be useful in helping with assessment and evaluation by observing children's reactions and engagement in the class. Areas you may want to evaluate include:

- Were the children engaged?
- Did we achieve the learning outcome?
- Did girls and boys engage equally with the activity?
- What do they need to learn next?

An example of a short questionnaire

One thing I liked was ...
One thing I didn't like was ...
One thing I have learned ...
One new skill I practised was ...
One thing I would like to know more about is ...

Or children could carry out an 'X marks the spot' exercise on a continuum:

Interesting...boring

For more ideas see the publication *Assessment, Evaluation and Sex and Relationships Education* (Blake and Muttock 2004).

Methods for assessment and evaluation

There are a whole variety of methods of finding out children's views in order to assess and evaluate the learning such as:

- book making (information books made by pupils for school library on such things as feelings, etc.)
- collages, displays and graffiti sheets
- crosswords (made by pupils for other pupils)
- dictionary making (words to do with PSHE and SRE and their meaning)
- hot seating – where children are asked to take on a role and then answer questions about themselves in that role
- individual records/reflections
- observation
- picture drawing – drawing or colouring in smiling or sad faces
- role-play and scenarios
- problem-solving
- questionnaires and quizzes
- record books
- word searches
- focus-group discussions.

This feedback should be attached to the lesson plan for future work, and could also be passed on to other staff members involved in SRE during team meetings. These methods also enable children to consolidate their own learning.

4 Content: Themes and outcomes

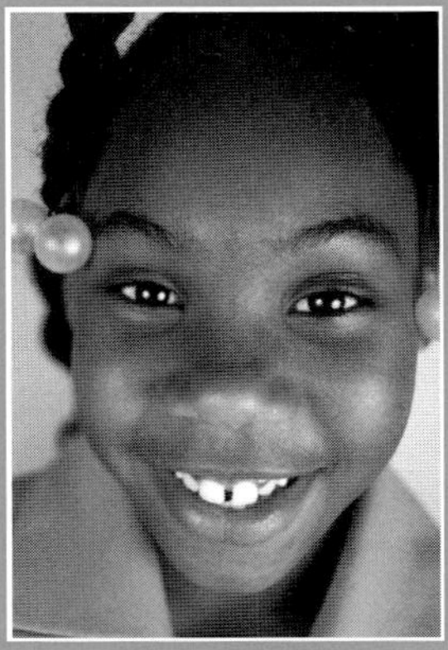

4 Content: Themes and outcomes

This section sets out eleven themes that provide the basis of an effective and comprehensive SRE programme. The themes are followed by expected learning outcomes for Key Stages 1 and 2, and a brief summary of why each theme should be included within the SRE programme.

These themes and learning outcomes have been developed by bringing together existing guidance into one coherent programme, that is from the:

- National Curriculum Science Programmes of Study (QCA 1999a) (Elements which must be covered as part of the National Curriculum are marked with an asterisk*)
- PSHE and Citizenship Framework (QCA 1999a)
- QCA Schemes of Work for Science – Unit 1A Ourselves (Growing and changing, similarities and differences), Unit 2A Health and Growth (Animals and humans produce young), Unit 4A Moving and Growing (Skeleton and parts of the body), Unit 5A (Life Cycles – adults have young, human babies are dependent on adults for an extended period) (QCA 1999b)
- Ofsted Learning Outcomes for SRE (2002).

Themes

- Male and female/body parts, reproduction and birth
- Growing and changing
- Similarities and differences
- Feelings
- Keeping safe
- Keeping yourself clean and healthy
- Someone to talk to
- Friends
- Families of all kinds
- Choices and consequences
- Gender stereotypes/Gender and sexuality

Note: Key Stage 1 does not cover 'birth' in theme 1; and in theme 11 it covers 'Gender stereotypes' rather than the 'Gender and sexuality' covered in Key Stage 2.

Male and female/body parts, reproduction and birth

By the end of Key Stage 1, the children should be able to recognise: the main external body parts of the bodies of humans*, that humans grow and reproduce*, that humans can produce offspring and that these grow into adults*; and recognise the differences between male and female humans and learn the agreed names of the sexual parts. They should also understand that babies, including animal babies, have mothers and fathers. (Note, birth itself is not covered at Key Stage 1.)

KS1

By the end of Key Stage 2, the children should: be able to identify parts of the reproductive system in males and females and describe their functions; have considered appropriate terminology for use in different contexts; know that life processes common to humans include growth and reproduction*; know about the main stages of the human life cycle*.

KS2

Body parts

Early and accurate naming of children's body parts is vital. Adult inhibitions about correct vocabulary may cause children to become confused about their bodies. Not knowing the words for parts of your body has serious implications for child protection, and in later years, conversations with the doctor and future partners. This is equally important for both boys and girls.

If children are to develop a positive sense of their bodies, sexual as well as reproductive body parts should be part of their vocabulary. Female body parts such as the clitoris and vulva are often not talked about in SRE, which could be due to teachers' and parents' anxieties. This absence can deprive girls of a conformable language about themselves.

Using accurate terminology consistently can also help staff feel more comfortable and confident in teaching about bodies. It is important to acknowledge that there are lots of other words that are used – so as not to embarrass children or undermine teaching at home – but also to emphasise what the correct words are and that they will be used within the school.

Reproduction

National Curriculum Science at Key Stage 1 requires that children develop an understanding that 'animals, including humans reproduce' and that 'humans produce babies and these babies grow into children and then into adults'. The SRE aspects of PSHE could include supportive work on the needs of children and families, parental responsibilities and how to get help.

During this time, children may ask questions such as: Do you *have* to have babies? Teachers can introduce the concept that adults can make decisions about whether or not to have a baby and answer questions in general terms. The responsibilities of parenthood and needs of very young children can be emphasised.

In Years 3 to 6, children are approaching or entering puberty. The Science Curriculum now requires teaching 'about the main stages of the human life cycle'. This involves an understanding of the beginning of fertility, and the process of contraception, which can be explained within a family context. Children will often have heard about contraception and may have seen contraception at home.

Work on friendships, relationships and morality, peer pressure, influence and making choices are all part of developing the skills children will need as they grow up. These skills are all-important for later teaching about contraception, as confidence and good self-esteem are fundamental to taking sexual and reproductive health issues seriously in the future.

Growing and changing

By the end of Key Stage 1, the children should understand how they have grown and changed since they were babies, and that they will go on growing and changing as they become adults; have thought about what babies need from parents or carers; and understand that animals, including humans, grow and reproduce*.

KS1

By the end of Key Stage 2, the children should have an understanding of puberty, reproduction and birth and have heard of contraception. They should understand that life processes common to humans and animals include growth and reproduction* and about the main stages of the human life cycle.

KS2

Preparing for puberty

All children need to be aware of, and have the skills to manage, both the physical and emotional changes relating to puberty (DfEE 2000). Many children grow up without any formal education about their bodies and the changes that take place. They also grow up without learning skills such as asking for help or without thinking about gender roles, expectations and relationships. Both boys and girls told us that they had anxieties and worries about their bodies. It is clear that primary schools have a key role in this and for supporting the children as these changes occur. Research shows that children cannot always rely on their parents who may not expect puberty to begin so early or might assume that it will be covered in school sessions.

> *Sex education is very important because at that stage of your life [puberty] it is like very exciting – but also you get very frightened, and if you don't know…*
>
> (Girl, Year 5)

> *I also knew about wet dreams so it wasn't a shock for me. I found out about these things from my older brother, but people without older brothers or sisters may have a big shock waiting for them.*
>
> (Boy, Year 6)

Teaching needs to include reassurance for both boys and girls that it is normal for the onset of puberty to vary widely and should include the preparation of early starters. Children also want an opportunity to discuss the emotional side of puberty. As one boy said, 'My sister's so moody now it's impossible to like her!' It is important to prepare children for the likely mood swings, feelings of confusion, embarrassment and shyness they may experience during puberty, without making it all sound gloomy and awful! How we do this carries significant messages both about how we value girls and boys and about their transition into adulthood.

Similarities and differences

By the end of Key Stage 1, the children should be able to understand similarities and differences between us* and about celebrating differences, treating others with respect* and gender stereotyping.

KS1

By the end of Key Stage 2, the children should be able to understand similarities and differences, respect each other and different viewpoints, challenge stereotypes; consider the diversity of lifestyles in our society; consider why being different can provoke bullying and why this is unacceptable; and see things from other people's points of view.

KS2

The fact that we are all the same in some ways yet different in others is a key piece of learning for children from the earliest years. Children can so easily pick up prejudiced attitudes based on lack of respect for people who are different from themselves from the world around them, sometimes at a very early age. Such attitudes are at the root of racism, homophobia and bullying. Primary schools can provide a role model for children by celebrating differences and teaching children the importance of being individuals. Linked to respect for differences is the concept of empathy and being able to see things from other people's point of view and understand why teasing and bullying are so hurtful.

Living in a multicultural and multi-faith society, we need to encourage children to understand other cultures and religions, and how attitudes and values relating to the family and sexual matters are similar or different to our own. Involving faith communities in the development of effective SRE is something which primary schools are well placed to do, since they often have good relations with parents and encourage them to come into school as much as possible (SEF 2004).

Feelings

By the end of Key Stage 1, the children should be able to recognise, name and deal with feelings; share them with other people; and feel positive about themselves. **KS1**

By the end of Key Stage 2, the children should be able to recognise changing emotions; develop confidence in facing new people and situations; feel positive about themselves; deal with stressful situations; and consider how their feelings and actions have an effect on other people. **KS2**

Feelings can be overwhelming at any age. Even knowing *what* it is we're feeling and then knowing how to behave appropriately is difficult for many adults. No wonder we often deny their importance and adopt the 'ostrich position'. So showing children that feelings have names, that we all have them and that they can be coped with – especially the difficult ones like anger and sadness – needs to be a vital part of anyone's emotional and social development.

Primary schools are places where children can learn that feelings are normal and can be managed – by listening to stories, doing activities where they can identify different feelings and by practising 'pretend' social situations. They will also see adults and hopefully their peers expressing and dealing with feelings in appropriate ways. Using children's literature is also a good way to focus on feelings in different situations.

Loss and bereavement can be a particularly difficult, although not uncommon, situation for schools to deal with and teach about, involving as it does acknowledging feelings, being able to talk, being able to listen and being aware of sources of help.

Keeping safe

By the end of Key Stage 1, the children should be able to recognise safe and unsafe situations, and know rules for keeping safe.

KS1

By the end of Key Stage 2, the children should be able to recognise risks, including peer pressure, and develop a range of strategies to keep themselves safe.

KS2

Personal safety is a key whole-school issue and strategies and skills for children can be learnt in PSHE and Citizenship. This work will include: recognising and identifying emotions such as feeling comfortable, uncomfortable, scared, unhappy; having a familiar vocabulary with which to describe their bodies; being able to identify a number of adults to turn to when in need (particularly important when one of this number may have abused their trust); learning assertiveness skills and knowing about privacy.

Given that children are more likely to be abused by someone known to them, it is important that this work doesn't focus too heavily on 'stranger danger'. Experience with children who have been asked to draw a stranger shows that 'stranger' is not a very meaningful concept for young children (they drew aliens and in one case an octopus!). A more useful approach might be to start with what makes children feel safe. Again, fiction can provide a safe way of providing opportunities to think about emotions and what to do if you feel unsafe.

Protective behaviours: One simple and effective technique used to support this work is called 'protective behaviours'. It enables children to identify and deal with any situation in which they do not feel safe and encourages young people to make their own decisions and take responsibility for these choices. The core principles include: 'We all have the right to feel safe all the time' and 'There is nothing so awful (or too little) we can't talk about it with someone.' The technique explores the following:

- **'unwritten rules'** that condition our thinking and behaviour, such as peer pressure
- **'thoughts, feelings and behaviour'** and their interrelationship, that is, that our feelings are neither right nor wrong but our behaviour, on the other hand, is a choice with an effect
- **'rights and responsibilities'** respecing both our own and other's rights (this includes, for instance, issues of coercion, bullying and abusive behaviour)
- **'feeling safe'** and how to trust intuitive and physical feelings (early warning signs)
- **'risking on purpose'** (when it feels scary and yet we want the outcome) while at the same time remembering others' right to feel safe with us
- **'support networks'** and how to build, use and maintain them.

Once the core process has been taught, children are encouraged to use the ideas to anticipate possible challenges and to practise problem-solving. This can be done in so many creative ways: through peer teaching, performance, creative writing, artwork, songs, and discussion for example.

Margetts and Lynch (2004)

Keeping yourself clean and healthy

By the end of Key Stage 1, the children should know the basic rules for keeping themselves safe and healthy, and be able to recognise the importance of good hygiene.

KS1

By the end of Key Stage 2, the children should know about the importance of personal hygiene, especially at puberty, and safe routines to stop the spread of infections and viruses (including HIV).

KS2

Any teacher will tell you that, despite all the advertisements on TV for soap and deodorant, there are many children who have not been shown the basics. Health professionals, too, know very well that ignorance of how infections are transmitted is often the contributing factor to a disease being contracted. This issue becomes especially important as children get closer to puberty. Primary schools need to ensure that personal cleanliness is included in the curriculum and pastoral care. A school nurse can often be a valuable ally in the classroom. This work will also help prepare the children for more in-depth work on HIV/AIDS and sexually transmitted infections in Key Stages 3 and 4.

Someone to talk to

By the end of Key Stage 1, the children should be able to know who they can talk to if they have a problem, and have the skills and confidence to talk about what's happening to them.

KS1

By the end of Key Stage 2, the children should know who they can talk to, feel confident to talk about problems, and know how to be a good listener.

KS2

Finding someone to talk to is often the next stage on from acknowledging feelings. Helping children to have the confidence to express themselves clearly is something which is at the heart of good primary practice anyway, but in SRE, schools can also ensure that children know who the best sources of help may be if they are worried or have a problem.

Discussions in class can help children identify who the 'people they trust' may be; and give extra information about local services, dependable helplines and websites (for example, the phone number for ChildLine, 0800 1111). Some schools also operate 'buddy schemes' where older pupils are trained to be listening ears for younger children.

Friends

By the end of Key Stage 1, the children should know about being a good friend, making friends, coping when friendships break down and dealing with bullying.

KS1

By the end of Key Stage 2, the children should be able to deal with conflict and bullying, know how to listen to and support friends, and manage friendship problems.

KS2

A good relationship is when the people who love each other are best friends as well.

(Boy, Year 5)

Work on friendships could be said to be the key to good SRE. If children are given opportunities to consider what makes a good friend and understand why they are attracted to some people rather than others, then they have the basis for developing good sexual relationships later on. This will also help with learning about empathy, being tolerant of differences and not having unrealistic expectations of others. Conflict resolution and dealing with bullying is something that all schools need to address.

Primary school teachers know that the ups and downs of friendships between children are the stuff of everyday life in school and that most children will have experienced many different aspects of friendship. Finding ways to discuss these things without using personal examples can be done in PSHE and SRE using children's literature, discussion, circle time, puppets, drama and case studies. All children should be aware of the school's anti-bullying strategy and where to go for help.

Families of all kinds

By the end of Key Stage 1, the children should understand how families care for us; and know how to cope with changes such as a new baby in the family, loss and bereavement.

KS1

By the end of Key Stage 2, the children should be able to understand that there are a wide range of family situations including marriage; why babies need families to love and care for them; and about divorce and separation, loss and bereavement.

KS2

Only six out of 32 children in my class live in a conventional family with both parents. If I went down the route of talking only about marriage I would not be addressing the needs of 26 of my pupils.

(Deputy headteacher)

Children need to have opportunities to explore different relationships – including families, friendships, partnerships and marriage – and by doing this to learn to value diversity. This is an area that children and young people report as often missing from their formal SRE (DfEE 2000). Children learn more about marriage and relationships from their own homes than they do from anywhere else (The National Society 2002) and these experiences provide powerful messages about how people manage relationships and behave towards others.

For some children, what they have learnt from their parents' or family members' relationships and marriages will be predominantly positive. 'For others it will be painful or unpredictable, confused and confusing. For some children, neglect or abuse will be what they know of relationships' (The National Society 2002). It is vital therefore, that schools should explicitly address this area of children's learning while showing sensitivity to different experiences.

SRE also needs to reflect the realities of children's very different lives. This will include children whose parents are married, those who are not married, children whose parents have divorced or separated, children in public care and children looked after by grandparents, mixed-race parents, disabled parents and same sex parents. Diverse family groupings should be represented and affirmed within the SRE resources used. In this respect, children's fiction is particularly useful.

> *Sometimes you can have two people who did love each other – but then they split up.*
>
> (Girl, Year 2)

> *My mum and dad did love each other. But now they're just friends because my dad lives somewhere else.*
>
> (Girl, Year 2)

> *How much more positive an experience it is for a child living with foster parents to experience 'the diversity of family life' as a starting point for an SRE discussion than the usual nuclear family starting point.*
>
> (Nurse for looked after children)

Choices and consequences

By the end of Key Stage 1, the children should be able to understand: that behaviour has consequences and that you can make choices; that feelings and actions have an impact on others. **KS1**

By the end of Key Stage 2, the children should be able to: understand that actions have consequences for themselves and other people; make good decisions and resist negative influences from peers and the media. **KS2**

SRE will provide much information for children about sensible and healthy behaviour. In order to be able to put this knowledge into practice, children need to have opportunities to practise making choices and decisions. The skills of decision-making involve being able to weigh up information, consider and resist pressures; being aware of the consequences of one's actions; as well as having the confidence and assertiveness to put the decisions into action.

There are many good PSHE and SRE resources that give children opportunities to consider a wide range of situations in which different choices can be made. Role-play, drama, case studies and 'problem page' answers can all be used effectively in the primary classroom (see Section 6 for details).

Gender and sexuality

By the end of Key Stage 1, the children should be able to reflect on the differences between boys and girls and think about whether girls and boys have to conform to gender stereotypes. **KS1**

By the end of Key Stage 2, the children should be able to challenge gender and sexual stereotypes.

KS2

Beginning to learn about gender equality and to challenge gender stereotypes is an important part of learning what it is to be a male or female in today's society and underpins choices children will make about relationships and sexuality as they grow up.

The lessons on gender stereotyping, for both Key Stages 1 and 2 in this resource, will help stimulate discussion of some of the issues.

However, the issues involved go far beyond the taught curriculum and must be addressed through the ethos and values of the school as a whole. Adults who work with children should be encouraged not to use gender stereotypes in their conversations with children, that is, to no longer say for example, 'Boys don't cry', 'I want a big strong boy to help me lift the equipment', 'Girls can't play football'. Make sure that you check through school and class libraries for books that encourage gender stereotyping and for books that present positive images of girls and boys, men and women in non-stereotypical roles. Find pictures of men and women doing non-stereotypical jobs and display these around the school. Encourage and comment on boys and girls who act outside the usual stereotypes. Make clear to parents through the school brochure and at parents' meetings that the school encourages boys and girls to take part in all activities equally.

5 Lesson plans

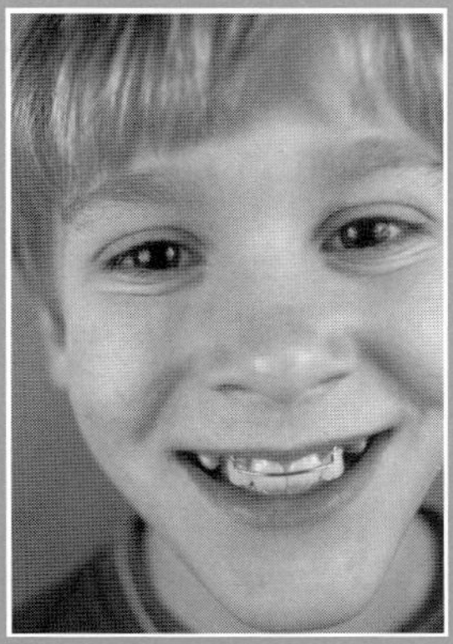

5 Lesson plans

These sample lesson plans provide ideas which can and should be adapted to the needs and values framework of each school. They reflect established good practice by integrating the biological elements in the National Curriculum Science and the emotional and social elements of SRE within the PSHE and Citizenship framework. It is the responsibility of the school to ensure that the activities you decide to use reflect your SRE policy.

The lessons follow the eleven themes outlined in the previous section (and summarised in Table 5.1). These lessons can be taught in any order; and schools will need to decide for themselves how they best fit into existing programmes of PSHE and Citizenship and how they meet the needs of the children. Teachers can mix and match activities from different themes, add their own ideas and omit things they do not like. There may also be opportunities to combine this work with the SEAL materials.

Working agreements

At the beginning of the programme, the children in the class should develop a working agreement. It should be written in child-friendly language and displayed in a prominent place. Rules should be referred to at the beginning of each lesson and will need to be reviewed and revised if and when necessary.

Example of a working agreement

We will try:

- to be kind to each other
- not to laugh at each other
- to listen to each other
- not to interrupt when someone else is speaking
- to respect other people's views
- to remember that we can always talk about things in private with the teacher
- to remember that we can always ask for help if we are worried about something.

Table 5.1 Key Stage 1

Lesson theme	At the end of this lesson children will:
Male and female	• be able to name the main external parts of the body • understand the differences between male and female, learn the agreed names of the sexual parts • understand that all babies, human and animal, have mothers and fathers.
Growing and changing	• understand how they have grown and changed since they were a baby and that they will go on growing and changing as they become adults.
Similarities and differences	• recognise similarities and differences between themselves and others • learn that their actions have an impact on other people • be able to identify ways in which they are special.
Feelings	• be able to recognise, name and deal with their feelings in a positive way • be able to share their feelings with others and realise that others have similar feelings • be able to think about themselves and recognise what they are good at.
Keeping safe	• be able to recognise safe and unsafe situations • be able to recognise the physical signs of feeling unsafe • know some basic rules for keeping themselves safe
Keeping yourself clean and healthy	• know and understand basic rules for keeping clean and healthy • understand that they have some control over the choices they make about looking after their body.
Someone to talk to	• be able to identify and talk with someone they trust.
Friends	• be able to make a friend, talk with them and share feelings • understand how their feelings and actions have an impact on other people.
Families of all kinds	• know and understand why families are special for caring and sharing • understand how their feelings and actions have an impact on other people.
Choices and consequences	• be aware that their feelings and actions have an impact on others • understand that they have some control over their actions.
Gender stereotypes	• recall the physical differences between boys and girls • be able to think about other 'differences' between girls and boys and where these (stereotypes) come from • begin to question whether children have to conform to gender stereotypes.

Male and female

KS1

In this lesson the children learn about body parts; talk about the differences between boy and girl babies; and match baby animals to their parents.

Learning objectives for this lesson

Children will:

- be able to name the main external parts of the body
- understand the differences between male and female, and learn the agreed names of the sexual parts
- understand that all babies, human and animal, have mothers and fathers.

You will need

- Body outline
- Labels with the correct names of body parts
- Pictures of babies
- Interactive whiteboard (if available)

Working agreement

Remind the children of the working agreement and emphasise that it's okay to laugh at something funny but not at another person.

A

Opening activity

Explain to the children that in this activity, you will ask them to move around the classroom. Then you will clap your hands and call a number and the name of part of the body (arms, legs, knees, fingers). At this, the children should join together in groups of the appropriate number with that part of their bodies touching. Now begin the activity.

Main activity

In a whole group or small groups, have a large sheet of paper with a body outline drawn on it (alternatively draw round a child). Ask the children to stick the prepared labels on appropriate parts of the body. Ask them if they know the names of any parts of the body that are inside (lungs, heart, stomach) and draw and label these. Alternatively you could use an interactive whiteboard for this activity, moving and placing labels for naming body parts.

Now show the children pictures of some babies with few or no clothes on. Talk to the children about what they think each baby is like and what they will be like as they grow up. Ask how we can tell whether each is a boy or a girl? Introduce words like *penis*, *testicles*, *vagina* and *womb* and explain that these are the parts which will mean that we can become a mother or a father when we grow up.

Show some pictures of animal babies and their adult parents, then match them into families while talking about the differences between male and female. Include a human trio.

Closing activity

Go round the class, asking each child in turn to complete the sentence 'Something I've learnt about bodies today is…'.

Sing a song about body parts such as *Head and shoulders, knees and toes* or *Dem Bones, dem bones*.

Additional activities

Make a wall display of animal babies and their parents. You may wish to use a video such as BBC's *Birth, Care and Growth* or C4's *Living and Growing Unit 1* (with resource book) to help you with these activities.

Additional resources

- Video: *Living and Growing Unit 1* (with resource book) (C4)
- Video: *Birth, Care and Growth* (BBC)
- Book: *My Body Your Body* (Manning and Granstrom 1999)

Differentiation

Children needing more of a challenge: could label the different organs in the body with their name and function, for example 'lungs – help you breathe', 'heart – pumps the blood'.

Children with additional learning needs: could match shapes and words pictorially. Give a line-drawing outline of a body on A3 paper, with outlines of major organs drawn in. Have words on cards that are the same shape as the organ. This reinforces knowledge of where these organs are in the body as well as encouraging word recognition.

Assessment

Collect children's 'home names' for their sexual body parts, for example *willy* and *boobs*, then ask them to match them up with the correct names to check their level of understanding.

What if…

…children get very giggly about names of sexual body parts or say that it's dirty to talk about them?

Remind them that people do often giggle if they are talking about something they don't usually talk about, but that it's really important to learn how your body works. Explain that all the parts of the body have an important job to do and that, though we generally keep them private, there's nothing bad about them.

Growing and changing

KS1

In this lesson the children bring in pictures of themselves or someone else as a baby and talk about what they needed when they were tiny and how they have changed.

Learning objectives for this lesson

Children will:

- understand how they have grown and changed since they were a baby and that they will go on growing and changing as they become adults.

You will need

- Photographs of babies (either ask the children to bring photos of themselves as babies or find some on the internet or in magazines) or ask a parent to bring a young baby in
- Whiteboard/flip chart
- Baby clothes and toys (children to bring some they had as babies or that belong to a baby they know)
- Babywear catalogues
- The book *The Baby's Catalogue* by Allan and Janet Ahlberg (if available)
- Glue and backing paper for making collages

Working agreement

Remind the children of the working agreement and focus on treating everyone kindly even if they are different from you.

A

Opening activity

In advance of this activity, ask children to bring in a picture of themselves or someone else as a baby. In class, invite them to talk about their photos in pairs and how they have changed since then. Alternatively, ask children to talk about their earliest memory or ask a parent to bring a young baby into the classroom.

Main activity

As a whole class, make a list of what the children can do now which they couldn't do when they were babies.

Ask the children to bring in clothes and toys that they had when they were a baby or that belong to a baby they know, and compare them with the ones they have now. You can also use babywear catalogues and look at the book *The Baby's Catalogue* by Allan and Janet Ahlberg. Create a time line, perhaps a collage using pictures from the catalogues to show the developing skills as we grow from a baby, to a toddler, to a Key Stage 1 child.

Closing activity

Ask the children to think about what might happen to them when they are grown up – that is, complete the sentence 'When I'm grown up I will…'.

Additional activities

Activity 1 You could also bring photos of yourself as a baby and at different stages through your life and discuss them with the class.
Activity 2 Some children in the class are likely to have experienced the arrival of a new baby.
This is a good opportunity to discuss the joys and difficulties of this new addition to the family. Start a discussion after reading a storybook which features a new baby in the family and ask the children to list the good things and the difficult things faced by older siblings and to suggest ways they can try and overcome the difficulties. Other children may want to talk about their experiences of the arrival of a new step sibling.

Additional resources

- Book: *Dr Xargle's Book of Earthlets* by J Willis and T Ross.
- Websites: UNICEF and Save the Children also have a range of materials on children's rights and needs – see website details in Section 6.

Differentiation

Children needing more of a challenge: could work on a time line showing the developing skills of a baby, using line drawings or cuttings from a magazine.

For example 'eating and drinking' could be illustrated thus:

breastfeeding > bottle feeding > cup with spout > being fed with spoon > independent use of cup > independent use of spoon and fork

And 'sleeping' like this:

in Moses basket > in cot > bed with cot sides > single bed

Children with additional learning needs: could work on a simplified time line (with only three to four stages) using line drawings or magazine cuttings. For example, like this:

newborn (in arms) > 6 months (sitting up) > 9 months (crawling) > 1 year (walking)

Assessment

The time lines used for differentiated activities could also be used as an assessment tool.

What if...

...some children can't bring in a photograph?

Have some other pictures of babies available or let them talk about you as a baby (you could bring in photographs of yourself at various stages to help them with this).

Similarities and differences

KS1

In this lesson the children talk about what is different and special about themselves, and learn that we can all help people feel good about themselves by being kind.

Learning objectives for this lesson

Children will:

- recognise similarities and differences between themselves and others
- learn that their actions have an impact on other people
- be able to identify ways in which they are special.

You will need

- Materials for drawing or painting portraits or writing materials
- Storybooks (e.g. *Elmer the Elephant*) or puppets

Working agreement

Remind the children of the working agreement and emphasise the need to treat everyone with respect.

A

Opening activity

Invite the children to form a circle, then ask them to stand up and change places if they have long/short hair, shoes with Velcro/buckles, like the colour blue/pink, have a birthday in a certain month and so on. Invite the children to form pairs, then ask them to find out two things they have in common and two things that are different and tell the rest of the group about them. (For example, 'We both have blue eyes but I am right-handed and you are left-handed.') Comment on how there are lots of ways that we are the same but lots of ways that we are special and different from each other.

Main activity

Get the children to draw or paint portraits of each other making them as detailed as possible. Alternatively, you could get them to write down a description. Then ask the children whether they can identify others from the portraits or descriptions. Stress that we are all unique and there is no-one else quite like us. You could invite them to go on to think about the ways in which we are the same (for example, we all need food and drink and sleep, we all feel sad if someone is nasty to us, we all like to play).

Read a story (such as *Elmer the Elephant*) or work with the children to make up a scenario about a puppet who is different because of the way 'he' or 'she' looks (for example, because they have glasses, freckles or are small/tall). Talk about how the character feels when people are nasty to them because they're different.

Play the guessing game using descriptions of children's characters, not physical attributes, for example: I'm kind, I help out in class, I smile a lot, and I like to talk, who am I?

Closing activity

Go round the class asking children to complete the sentence 'I'm proud of being different because…', or 'I'm special because…', or 'I like the person next to me because…'.

Additional activities

Activity 1 Write each child's name on a piece of paper. Hand out the pieces of paper to the class randomly. Ask each child to write something positive about the child whose name they've got. Fold up the pieces of paper and put them in a box. Take one piece out each day and read the comment to the class.

Activity 2 As an alternative, give each child an A4 sheet of paper and ask them to write their name at the top. Pass the sheets around and invite each child to write a positive comment at the bottom of the sheet about the person whose name is at the top. After writing their comment, get them to fold up the sheet, so that the comment is hidden, before passing it on to the next child.

Activity 3 Use ICT to create a database in a program such as 'information workshop' or '2Investigate' to explore similarities and differences.

Differentiation

Children needing more of a challenge: could write detailed descriptions of each other's appearance and characteristics.

Children with additional learning needs: could use mirrors to help make accurate representations of their faces. They can then use digital cameras to compare and contrast their images.

Assessment

Ask the children to complete sentences such as:

- In the lesson, I learnt that…
- One thing that is special about me is…
- It is good to say positive things to others because…

What if…

…there is a child in the class who is often picked on because of their appearance?

Make sure you remind the class of the working agreement throughout the activities. Distance the learning by focusing on the book character or puppet and getting the children to think about how it feels to be laughed at.

Feelings

KS1

In this lesson the children explore a range of uncomfortable and positive emotions and think about how their actions cause feelings in others. Teachers will find further ideas and resources for tackling this theme in the SEAL materials (DfES 2005).

Learning objectives for this lesson

Children will:

- be able to recognise, name and deal with their feelings in a positive way
- be able to share their feelings with others and realise that others have similar feelings
- be able to think about themselves and recognise what they are good at.

You will need

- Noisy musical shaker
- Whiteboard or flip chart
- Soft toy or puppet

Working agreement

Remind the children about the working agreement and emphasise the importance of listening to others.

A

Opening activity

Play the silent rattle: invite the children to form a circle, then pass a tambourine, maracas or set of bells around the class asking the children to make as little noise as possible. At the end of the round, ask them how they felt as the instrument came towards them. You can write all the feelings on a whiteboard or flip chart.

Use the circle of feelings: Introduce the children to the idea of a 'circle of feelings', which is when you record, on the whiteboard or flip chart, the children's feelings at different times throughout the day or week. Use a different coloured pen each time you add words. At the end of the day or week, discuss with the class how our feelings change and what makes them change.

Main activity

Pick one of the words from the silent rattle activity (above), such as *nervous* or *scared*. Ask them to think about other times when they have felt like that and, for example, to finish the sentence: 'I feel scared when…'. Emphasise the fact that they have all felt the same at some time or another.

Alternatively, using a soft toy or puppet, name a feeling word (try to avoid obvious words like sad and happy) and ask the children to describe what is making him or her feel like that. (For example: *lonely* – I think Rabbit is feeling lonely because his mum has gone to work; or *excited* – I think Rabbit is feeling excited because he's going on holiday.) Continue by asking children what makes them feel like that. End with a negative feeling and ask children what they could do to make Rabbit feel better.

Draw a body outline on a whiteboard or flip chart. Ask the children to talk about how different feelings make their body react on the outside (posture and verbal expressions such as smiling laughing, sighing or groaning) and on the inside (breathing, heartbeat, wobbly knees, hot or cold, goose bumps, butterflies in the tummy, warm glow all over).

Closing activity

In the circle, ask individual children to move across the circle as if they were feeling a particular emotion (proud, miserable, excited). You could make it into a guessing game. Look back at the 'circle of feelings' (the Opening activity) and reflect on the range of feelings experienced during the day or week.

Additional activities

It is impossible to cover many different feelings in one lesson. Ideally, the work on feelings will be an ongoing part of the PSHE and Citizenship programme and will link to literacy by building up 'feelings' word banks and exploring the feelings of characters in stories.

Differentiation

Children needing more of a challenge: could use word cards with 'feeling' words on and photo cards with facial expressions on, to discuss a range of emotions (upset, angry, annoyed and so on). They could then make sentences starting 'I was annoyed when…'.

Children could choose a piece of music or paint an abstract picture depicting an emotion (such as angry, happy, sad).

Children with additional learning needs: could concentrate on a few feelings such as happy, sad, angry or worried, then practise recognising the facial expressions for each of them. They could take digital photos and use them for a guessing game.

Make masks on a stick. Illustrate each feeling and make up a story with the children holding up the masks at appropriate places.

Assessment

Listen and observe the children throughout, note any children who find it hard to put feelings into words and consider whether they need follow-up activities in this area.

What if...

...children find it very hard to come up with words for feelings?

Plan in some more work for the class on this topic and look for additional resources.

Keeping safe

KS1

In this lesson the children think about all the things they have to keep safe from, and come up with some basic rules for keeping safe.

Learning objectives for this lesson

Children will:

- be able to recognise safe and unsafe situations
- be able to recognise the physical signs of feeling unsafe
- know some basic rules for keeping themselves safe.

You will need

- Large body outline
- Material for making a collage (glue, backing paper, scissors or paint/coloured pens)

Working agreement

Remind the children about the working agreement and remind them in particular that some things may be better talked about in private than with the whole class. Make sure they know when they can come and talk to you in private.

A

Opening activity

Use a 'draw and write' activity: invite the children to draw a picture of themselves feeling and keeping safe. Then ask them to write what they have done to keep safe.

Alternatively, ask the children to form a circle. Then ask: How do you feel when you are safe and where do you feel safest? Invite each child in turn to give their answer, for example by completing the sentence 'I feel really safe when…'.

Then talk about all the things which scare us and which we need to keep safe from. For example, each child in turn could complete the sentence 'I sometimes feel scared when…'.

Make sure you distinguish between real and imaginary dangers and finish by talking about, or reminding them of, things that they said made them feel safer.

Main activity

Warning signs

Build on the work on feelings in the last lesson. Using a large body outline, invite children to think about what happens to their bodies when they know they are in an unsafe situation. To help them, give them some scenarios (someone being unkind to them, getting lost, going somewhere or doing something they don't want to do) and draw on the physical signs of feeling unsafe (heart beating fast, wobbly knees, butterflies in the tummy, heavy feeling, hunched shoulders and such like). These are their 'let's get out of here' signs, a warning that they may be in an unsafe situation and need to do something to keep themselves safe. This is a good opportunity to use drama to look at different body language and personal space.

Keeping safe with people

Create a whole-class collage to show all the people who can help keep us safe, for example families including pets, friends, grown-ups, and people whose job it is to keep us safe. Add the captions 'Who can help me keep safe?' and 'What do they do to keep me safe?'

Keeping ourselves safe

Remind the children of all the ways they said they were changing since they were babies. Add that one of the ways they are changing is that they are now getting old enough to help keep themselves safe. Get them to come up with a class list, or display, of all the ways they can do this. (For example: ask a grown-up, hold their hand, think before rushing off, handle scissors and knives carefully, listen to their warning signs and – the main rule (at this age) – *tell a trusted adult if anything is making you feel unsafe.*) Theme 7 'Someone to talk to' deals with identifying appropriate adults to talk to.

Good/safe and bad/unsafe touches

Talk about how people who love and care for us make us feel safe – with hugs and cuddles and kisses. Think about people who we wouldn't be happy to hug and cuddle us – strangers, people we don't know well. Stress that nobody has the right to touch our bodies, especially the sexual private parts, even people we like and know if we don't want them to, especially if we are getting warning signs that we don't feel safe. Tell them that if anyone, even if it is someone they know, tries to touch them in a way that makes them feel unsafe they must tell another adult. You may want to talk about nurses and doctors who may need to touch them all over to find out if anything is wrong.

Closing activity

Play Fruit salad: end the lesson with this fun circle game to remind us that we can all help to keep each other safe. Go round the circle allocating each child the name of a fruit – apple, orange or banana. Explain that when you call out the name of a fruit – all the children with that name should stand up and move across the circle to find another seat. And that when you call out 'Fruit salad', all the children should stand up and change places. Before you start the game discuss what might happen if all the children ran across the circle and ask the children to come up with some rules that will help everyone keep safe during the game. Praise them when you see them following their rules and being careful not to hurt anyone else.

Pass a smile or hand squeeze round the circle.

Differentiation

Children needing more of a challenge: could make a 'keeping safe' book listing dangerous activities and how to keep yourself safe.

Children with additional learning needs: could work with the learning assistant to create a group display showing ways to keep safe.

Note: The concept of 'safe' is difficult for some younger children to grasp. This needs to be kept in mind and reinforced at regular intervals.

Assessment

In a circle, ask the children individually to complete the sentence: 'Now I am growing up, I can keep myself safe by…'.

Note their responses and reflect on whether they need to do any further work on this topic.

What if…

…a child discloses that someone at home has made them feel unsafe?

Don't dismiss what they have said but gently follow up on the working agreement by saying that this is something the child could talk to you about in private after the lesson. Find a time to talk to them as soon as possible, praise them for being brave enough to tell you, do not promise confidentiality, and say you will try to get someone to help them. Follow the school's Child Protection Procedures.

Keeping yourself clean and healthy

In this lesson the children play a game to get them to think about keeping clean, then discuss what is good and bad for their health.

Learning objectives for this lesson

Children will:

- know and understand basic rules for keeping clean and healthy
- understand that they have some control over the choices they make about looking after their bodies.

You will need

- Body outline
- Objects for Kim's Game
- The book *A Piece of Cake* by Jill Murphy

Working agreement

Remind children about the working agreement and emphasise that it is okay to laugh at something funny but not at another person.

A

Opening activity

Play Kim's game: put a number of objects related to keeping clean and healthy on a tray (soap, toothbrush, toothpaste, apple, carrot, towel, tissue and so on). Remove one object at a time (under a cloth so the children can't see) and get them to remember which object is missing. You could also include an 'odd one out' such as a sweet. At the end, ask the children if they can think what all the objects have in common and discuss why each one is important and why it is important to keep clean and healthy.

Alternatively, put all the objects in a bag or box and get children to take turns to take one out and say why we need it.

Main activity

Using a body outline to record their ideas, get the children to brainstorm all the things that go into our bodies and how they get in. Divide the things into two categories: things they think are 'good for the body' and those they think are 'bad for the body'. Introduce the idea of germs that get into the body and cause illnesses. What can we do to prevent the bad things getting into the body? Make a class list of rules around the body outline (for example, don't smoke, don't eat too many sweets, wash your hands, go to the dentist). You could also ask the children if they have had any injections and what they were for, then add to the list 'Go to the doctor to have your injections.'

Talk about who is responsible for making healthy choices and how this changes as we grow up – mostly it's the adults that care for them, but now they are getting older they can decide too. Make a class list of healthy decisions they can make to keep themselves healthy and clean.

Closing activity

Go round the class asking children to complete the sentence 'One thing I'm going to do to keep myself clean and healthy is…'.

Read *A Piece of Cake* by Jill Murphy. Talk about how difficult it can be to try and always be healthy.

Differentiation

Children needing more of a challenge: could increase the number of objects or add unfamiliar items or give time limits in Kim's Game – or do all of these.

Encourage them to think about the different ways things get into our bodies, such as: through our mouths – food, water, medicine; our noses – breathing air, germs, and so on.

Children with additional learning needs: could reduce the number of objects in Kim's game.

Or they could use the outline of the missing object (a visual clue) to assist them with matching and memory, and work in pairs.

Assessment

Using two line drawings of a child's body – one with a happy face and one with a sad face – and write over the top the titles 'Things that are good for my body' and 'Things that are not so good for my body'.

Note: Avoid the word **bad** as, especially in the case of food, there are no bad foods, just foods that we are trying to discourage children from eating every day.

Give the children lists or pictures cut from magazines – which could include soap, toothpaste, shampoo, pop, sweets, fruit, water, cigarettes, burgers, chips, and vegetables – and ask them to place them on the appropriate line drawings.

What if…

…there is a child in the class who is often dirty and smelly?

Remind the class of the working agreement about treating each other kindly. The school should be contacting the parents or carers about this problem. Maybe the school nurse, learning mentor or home school liaison worker could help by talking to the child and their family. Some schools have a supply of spare clothes to lend out if necessary.

Someone to talk to

KS1

In this lesson the children talk about why they might need someone to confide in and make their own list of people they can trust.

Learning objectives for this lesson

Children will:

- be able to identify and talk with someone they trust.

You will need

- Cushions or other soft objects for obstacles
- Puppet
- Coloured paper, pens/crayons, scissors
- Book *Not Now Bernard* by David McKee

Working agreement

Remind children about the working agreement and emphasise that it's okay to ask for help.

A

Opening activity

Play the Trust game: ask the children to form a circle, then put 'obstacles' such as cushions in the middle. Blindfold one of the children and ask another to lead them across the circle around the obstacles. Repeat with other children taking the roles of leader and blindfolded follower. Discuss how it feels to need help and to have someone help you. Talk about how you need to be able to trust them.

Alternatively, ask children to work in pairs to share their ideas on 'things we need someone's help with' or 'why it's good to have someone you can talk to'. Go round and ask each pair to tell the class what their ideas were.

Main activity

Use a puppet or soft toy to 'say' that they want to tell you something that has been worrying them but that they are scared and do not quite know how to say it. Get the children to give the puppet encouragement to tell you. The puppet might tell you, for example:

- that someone has been bullying him/her
- that he/she is worried about their sister/brother
- that he/she doesn't understand their maths
- that he/she is worried they have lost their reading book.

Get the children to ask questions to help the puppet explain what is the matter. Then get them to think about what they would do if the puppet asked them for help.

Talk about the people children could talk to if they need help or have a problem. Play Helping hands: give each child a piece of coloured paper to draw round their hand. Then ask them to write the name of an adult they can talk to on each finger and cut it out to take home.

Make sure that you tell them they can always come to you and tell you what is worrying them. Some teachers have a 'worry box' for children to communicate with them or set up a special time when children know they can come and talk.

Closing activity

Read *Not Now Bernard* by David McKee. Then go round the class asking children to complete the sentence 'If I were Bernard I would…'.

Pass a smile or hand squeeze round the class.

Differentiation

Children needing more of a challenge: could work in twos to make up a play using two puppets, taking one of the examples from the main activity section.

Children with additional learning needs: could do further role play with the puppet, explaining that it is okay to ask for help and suggesting people who could help.

Assessment

Ask children to indicate whether they think they have learnt a lot (thumbs up), a bit (thumbs horizontal) or only a little (thumbs down). Ask for another show of thumbs in response to 'how much you enjoyed the lesson' and 'how well you think you all cooperated and worked together'.

What if...

...a child does not live with their parents?

Make sure that children who do not live with their parents still feel included by suggesting a wide range of people they could go to for help.

Friends

KS1

In this lesson each child finds out something about another class member and thinks about what makes a good friend. They then act out responses to situations in which friends fall out.

Learning objectives for this lesson

Children will:

- be able to make a friend, talk with them and share feelings
- understand how their feelings and actions have an impact on other people.

You will need

- Paper and drawing materials for posters
- Puppet or soft toy

Working agreement

Remind the children of the working agreement and emphasise the importance of treating each other kindly.

A

Opening activity

Play the 'I'd like to tell you about' game: in a circle, divide the children into pairs (pairing children who do not usually mix together). Give the pairs a set time (3 to 5 minutes) for each member to find out three things that the other really likes. Then each child introduces their partner to the whole group starting with 'I'd like to tell you about [*insert name*].' Comment on the number of similarities and differences between the children in the class. Then ask for answers to 'Why is it good to have friends?' and discuss.

Main activity

Ask children to think about what makes a good friend. Either as a class, groups or individuals create a 'Wanted' poster for a Good Friend.

Ask: What happens to make friends fall out? What can you do when this happens? Discuss their responses.

Use puppets to act out a situation in which two friends fall out. Ask: What can they do to become friends again? (For example, say sorry, say you didn't mean to hurt them, do something kind for them.)

Alternatively, ask children in groups to create a frozen image of a situation where two friends have had an argument. Talk about their body language, their thoughts and feelings, and what they can do to make up and how other children could help.

Closing activity

Go round the class asking children to complete the sentence 'Something I've learnt about friends today is…'.

Differentiation

Children needing more of a challenge: could develop a word board, for example on what makes a good friend. Get children to suggest words as well as having some of your own, such as, happy, funny, kind, nice, plays with me, and shares.

Children with additional learning needs: could use photo cards of different types of body language (these can be bought commercially or you could make your own with the children posing for camera shots), such as turning away, avoiding eye contact, crossing their arms, yawning, frowning, smiling. Discuss in small groups. Ask: Does this person look like a good friend?

Assessment

Observe children throughout the activities and listen carefully to their responses to the closing activity. Reflect whether the learning objectives have been met.

What if…

…children start arguing about an incident that happened at playtime?

Say that you will deal with the situation after the lesson and remind them of the working agreement.

Families of all kinds

KS1

In this lesson the children talk about the special people in their lives and learn how to get over arguments at home. They will touch on loss and bereavement.

Learning objectives for this lesson

Children will:

- know and understand why families are special for caring and sharing
- understand how their feelings and actions have an impact on other people.

You will need

- Whiteboard or flip chart

Working agreement

Remind the children of the working agreement and emphasise that we are all special and should listen to each other.

A

Opening activity

Brainstorm: invite responses from all the children on 'who our special people are'. Record all the children's answers in a circle, on a whiteboard or flip chart, so that they all seem to be equal.

Main activity

Ask the children: How do our special people show they love and care for us? Invite them to illustrate their answers then use their pictures and captions to create a wall display (including, for example, a picture of a child's grandmother alongside the caption 'She cooks me a nice dinner'; or a little brother with 'He hugs me').

Then ask: How do *we* show we care for our special people? Discuss the responses then add their comments or illustrations to the display.

Ask the children: What do we do to upset our special people? What might happen then? Talk about arguments and people getting cross, including siblings or other children, and talk about why this happens (for example, adults get tired, it's hard to share). Let children know that all families quarrel from time to time. As with the lesson on 'Friends', talk about ways to make up and get on again. Remind the children that if they are worried about something that's happening at home they can always talk to you.

Talk about how we feel if we can't see one of our special people for a while and how we can keep in touch with or remember them by phoning, emailing, texting, sending cards or keeping something special to remind us of them. Be sensitive to the fact that there may be a restraining order on a parent or relative so check before encouraging them to phone or email, also be sensitive to any child who has had a bereavement.

Closing activity

Go round the class asking children to complete the sentence 'Something I'm going to do for one of my special people to show them I care about them is...'

Additional resources

Books: stories about families, such as *Billy and Belle* by Sarah Garland (Puffin)

Book: *Childhood Bereavement: Developing the curriculum and pastoral support* by Nina Job and Gill Frances

Differentiation

Children needing more of a challenge: could design and write a greeting card to say thank you to one of their special people for everything they do to help and look after them.

Children with additional learning needs: could design a card as above and dictate the greeting to the learning assistant to type and print on the computer, or choose a ready printed greeting.

Assessment

Observe the activities closely and reflect on how the children responded. Decide whether they need further work on this topic.

What if...

...a child gets very upset because their parents have just split up?

Tell them that it is okay to feel sad and remind them of other special people in their lives. Tell them that it is good to talk about feelings and let them know that you will always try to find time to listen. You may be able to find another child in the school who has gone through the same experience who could be a special buddy. You could also find a storybook about children whose parents split up.

Choices and consequences

KS1

In this lesson the children see puppets acting out a scene where someone is unkind to someone else. Then they think of times when they have been angry or unkind themselves and think of things they could do to make someone feel better. Calming techniques are also introduced.

Learning objectives for this lesson

Children will:

- be aware that their feelings and actions have an impact on others
- understand that they have some control over their actions.

You will need

- Puppets
- Whiteboard/flip chart

Working agreement

Remind the children about the working agreement and emphasise the rule about treating each other with respect.

A

Opening activity

Play Fruit salad: get the children to sit in a circle and give each the name of one of three fruits (for example apple, orange, banana). Tell them that when you call out a fruit, all the children with that name should stand up and change places; and when you say 'fruit salad' everyone should stand up and change places. Ask children what might happen when you call 'fruit salad' (people might push and shove and someone might get hurt) and how they can prevent this happening. Ask them to see if they can come up with, and follow, their own rules. Praise them for choosing to behave sensibly.

Main activity

Use two puppets, A and B, to enact a scenario where A has been unkind to B for example by not letting him or her join in a game. Get the children to think about how B is feeling. Ask them to tell A how he has made his friend feel and what they think he should do. Get A to tell the children (through you) that he didn't realise that he had hurt B so much.

Ask the children to be very honest and tell the class about a time when they were unkind to someone (no names to be mentioned). Praise their honesty and say the most important thing is to see what you've done wrong and try to put it right. Ask them how they know that someone is feeling hurt. Get them to brainstorm a list of kind things we can do to make others feel better when we see that they are feeling hurt.

Get the children to brainstorm times when they have felt very angry with another person. Talk about how it feels inside when you are angry. Ask: What do you feel like doing when you are angry? (For example, hitting out, shouting at them, breaking something?) What happens if you do that? (Answers could include: someone gets hurt, a fight starts.) Teach them a calming technique (such as counting to 10, taking some deep breaths, walking away) so that they see they have time to decide calmly what to do next.

Closing activity

Go round the class asking children to complete the sentence 'When I feel mad with someone, it helps me control my behaviour if…'.

Additional resources

Book: *Angry Arthur* by Oram Hiawyn and Satoshi Kitamuri

Differentiation

Children needing more of a challenge: could complete the following sentences to show the consequences of certain actions.

- If you push and shove others…
- If you shout at other people…
- If you are rude to other people…
- If you fight other people…
- If you are kind to other people…
- If you smile at other people…
- If you help other people…

Children with additional learning needs: could do further role-play work with the puppet exploring similar situations to those above.

Assessment

Listen carefully to children's responses to the closing activity.

Ask them to tell you one thing they've learnt today.

Ask them what they liked and didn't like about the activities.

What if…

…children suggest that puppet A should hit puppet B?

Get the puppet to talk into your ear and tell the children that he said he has tried hitting back before but that it ended up in a fight and he got hurt so he doesn't think that's a good idea.

Gender stereotypes

KS1

In this lesson the children are reminded of the physical differences between boys and girls and go on to discuss other differences between the sexes and whether these are inevitable. They then discuss qualities that boys and girls have in common.

Learning objectives for this lesson

Children will:

- recall the physical differences between boys and girls
- be able to think about other 'differences' between girls and boys and where these (stereotypes) come from
- begin to question whether children have to conform to gender stereotypes.

You will need

- Large picture of a baby
- Whiteboard or flip chart
- Paper, pencils and colouring materials
- Toy catalogue or pictures of toys
- Scissors
- Story books: *The Paper Bag Princess* by Robert Munsch, Scholastic; *Happy Familes* Series by Allan Ahlberg, Young Puffin Books (especially *Mrs Plug the Plumber*, *Mrs Wobble the Waitress*, *Mr Biff the Boxer* and *Miss Jump the Jockey*)

Working agreement

Remind the children of the working agreement and emphasise the importance of listening carefully to each other and respecting different viewpoints.

A

Opening activity

Find a picture of a baby whose gender is not immediately obvious. Ask the children to suggest a name for the baby. They could do this in pairs, small groups or you could take suggestions from the whole group. If they ask 'Is the baby a boy or a girl?', tell them you don't know. If they simply suggest names, ask them why they are assuming that it is a boy or a girl (there will probably be some statements made here that you can explore later in the lesson). Remind them of what they learnt in the lesson on Male and Female. A simple explanation would be:

> A girl's body has a vagina behind the little hole where she pees from and inside her tummy there is a special place where babies can grow when she is older. This means she will be able to be a mother when she is grown up.

A boy's body has a penis and testicles which produce sperm that can help make a baby when he is older. This means he will be able to be a father when he is grown up. A boy also pees out of his penis.

Show the children some pictures of male and female babies as in the lesson on Male and Female.

Main activity

Explain to the class that you are now going to think about whether there are any other differences between boys and girls apart from the physical ones we are born with.

You can either do this as a whole class brainstorm or divide the children into small groups. Ask them to think about whether there are any other differences between boys and girls. Write these on the board, or get the children to note down their ideas as they talk in their group to give as feedback to the whole class. You will probably get responses similar to the following:

Girls have long hair/boys have short hair.
Girls wear skirts and dresses/boys wear trousers.
Girls like pink/boys like blue.
Girls play with dolls/boys play with cars.
Girls get scared and cry/boys are brave.
Girls are gentle/boys are rough.

Then lead a whole class discussion on where young babies learn that boys and girls behave in certain ways and whether they have to be like that as they grow up. Challenge the children's views gently, by asking for example: Do girls have to have long hair? Do all boys have to like playing football? Aren't boys ever scared? Can't girls be brave? Can't boys be gentle? You can also ask everyone to put up their hand if they like playing in the role-play area. You won't be able to challenge all their statements. The aim is simply to show that there are alternative viewpoints and that children can choose how they behave. You can also ask the class how it is that children learn about these differences in the way boys and girls behave and look like.

Then ask the children about the things that boys and girls have in common and can both do equally well. For example ask them:

- Do both boys and girls like watching television?
- Do both boys and girls like chips and sweets?
- Do both boys and girls get sad sometimes?
- Can both boys and girls try hard at their work?
- Can both boys and girls be brave?
- Can both boys and girls be kind and helpful?

Write their answers up on the board.

Closing activity

Read the children a story which challenges gender stereotypes, such as the *Paperbag Princess* or any of the Ahlberg's *Happy Families* series and talk about how the characters are behaving in a way that we might not expect a male or a female to behave.

Additional activity

You could extend the discussion in the main activity into a wider discussion about men and women and their different roles – particularly around the house and in caring for children – and to the different jobs men and women do. Try to challenge the children's views that these differences are inevitable and be ready to suggest jobs that are done by both sexes (such as bus drivers, soldiers, astronauts, postal deliveries, nurses, doctors).

Differentiation

Children needing more of a challenge: design a birthday card that would be suitable for a boy and a girl.

Children with additional learning needs: could work with a teaching assistant or other helper to look through a toy catalogue and choose and cut out pictures of toys that boys and girls would both enjoy playing with. At the same time they could continue talking about differences and similarities.

Assessment

Listen carefully to the children's responses to the questions you ask them and assess whether they are able to begin to question stereotypical views. If more work is needed, assess whether you need to do this in lessons or through daily interactions in the classroom (by commenting on non-stereotypical behaviour and challenging stereotypes wherever possible).

Go round the class asking each child to complete the sentence 'Something I have learnt about boys and girls is …'.

What if…

…a child comments 'My dad says that boys don't cry'?

Explain that anyone might cry if they get hurt or feel very sad or upset and that crying is a natural way of showing your feelings. Ask the children if there is anyone who has never cried. Explain that there are some people who think that boys and men should always be strong and never show if they are hurt or sad, but that it is perfectly natural to cry, that it will help you start to feel better and that if other people see you crying they will know you need help.

Table 5.2 Key Stage 2

Lesson theme	By the end of the lesson children will:
Male and female	• be able to identify parts of the reproductive system in males and females and describe their functions • have considered appropriate terminology for use in different contexts.
Reproduction and birth	• know and understand about the processes of reproduction and birth as part of the human life cycle • understand what babies need in order to be happy and healthy • understand the demands of looking after a baby • think about how they can help care for babies and young children they know.
Growing and changing: puberty	• know and understand about the physical changes that take place at puberty • recognise and understand changing emotions as they grow up.
Similarities and differences	• be able to respect other people's viewpoints and beliefs • be able to see things from other people's viewpoints • have considered why being different can provoke bullying and why this is unacceptable • be able to express opinions for example about relationships and bullying.
Feelings	• recognise changing emotions with friends and family and be able to express their feelings positively • be self-confident in a range of situations • recognise their own worth and identify positive things about themselves • be able to balance the stresses of life in order to promote both their own mental health and well-being and that of others.
Keeping safe	• know and understand about keeping themselves safe when involved with risky activities • recognise the pressure of unwanted physical contact and know ways of resisting it • understand when it is appropriate to take a risk and when to say no and seek help.
Keeping yourself clean and healthy	• know and understand that you have to take extra care with personal hygiene during puberty • know and understand that safe routines can stop the spread of viruses including HIV.
Someone to talk to	• be able to listen to and support others • be able to identify adults they can trust and who they can ask for help • be able to listen to and support their friends • know where individuals, families and groups can get help.
Friends	• be able to express opinions, for example about relationships and bullying • be self-confident in a wide range of situations, such as seeking new friends • manage friendship problems • understand about different forms of bullying and the feelings of both bullies and victims.
Families of all kinds	• be able to recognise their changing emotions towards their families • be able to see things from other people's viewpoints, for example their parents' and carers' • know and understand about the many relationships in which they are all involved • have considered the need for trust and love in established relationships • know and understand about, and accept, a wide range of different and diverse family arrangements, for example, married, divorced or separated parents, second marriages, fostering, extended families, same sex parents, and three or more generations living together • have considered how separation and loss affect people in the family.
Choices and consequences	• be able to form opinions which they can articulate to a variety of audiences • be able to discuss moral questions • know and understand that their actions have consequences and be able to anticipate the results of them • understand and be able to resist peer and media pressure.
Gender and sexuality	• be able to recognise and challenge gender stereotypes • have considered why being different can provoke bullying and why this is unacceptable • understand how the media impact on forming attitudes.

Male and female

KS2

In this lesson the children label a life-size diagram with the names of internal body organs. They look at drawings or diagrams of male and female reproductive organs and learn how they relate to things that will happen to them. They brainstorm names for sexual body parts, learn to understand what they mean and about their appropriate use.

Learning objectives for this lesson

Children will:

- be able to identify parts of the reproductive system in males and females and describe their functions
- have considered appropriate terminology for use in different contexts.

Note: You may need to check whether the representation of the human body is acceptable to parents of different faiths in the class. (Your school's SRE policy should address this.)

You will need

- Large sheets of paper and pens
- Accurate representation of male and female bodies including reproductive organs
- Interactive whiteboard (if available)

Working agreement

Remind the children about the working agreement, emphasise the importance of treating each other with respect and about the need to think before talking about personal matters with the whole group.

A

Opening activity

Draw round the outline of a child's body as a whole class or in groups, or use a ready prepared body outline. Ask children to draw in as many internal organs as they can. Talk them through the major body systems: respiratory, digestive, muscular-skeletal, immune, nervous, and reproductive. Stress what an extraordinary 'machine' the human body is, especially with regard to reproduction.

Main activities

You will need accurate representations of the human reproductive organs in males and females – make sure the children understand how they relate to the body as a whole (sometimes disembodied organs are difficult to understand). Many SRE packs, videos and anatomical models are available, or you can draw your own. Describe the functions of the different parts in the context of growing up and becoming an adult. Answer questions.

Brainstorm the words children know for sexual body parts and make sure they know how they relate to the correct medical terms – *vagina*, *womb*, *ovaries*, *fallopian tubes*, *clitoris*, *penis*, *testes*, *scrotum*, *urethra*. Talk about how we need to use different words in different situations and with different people – at home, in public places, at school, with health staff.

Closing activity

Give children a diagram of the reproductive organs and ask them to label the parts. You could do this as a quiz, then pass it to another group to mark.

Go round the class asking children to complete the sentence 'One thing I've learnt today that I didn't know before is…'.

Differentiation

Children needing more of a challenge: could make a body 'dictionary' with accurate descriptions of the functions of the major organs, including the reproductive system.

Children with additional learning needs: may find understanding the concept of 'what is inside our bodies' quite difficult, so you might want to work with small groups of children to explain it more fully. Make aprons with actual (child-) sized organs on (with adult support) as this enhances children's understanding of how things 'fit together' (you can also buy these from Science Education catalogues).

Assessment

Use pupil-made quizzes, as above.

What if…

…someone says, I've seen my dad's willy?

You'll probably want to refer to the point in the class working agreement about talking about personal matters. Point out to the class that talking about personal things isn't always a good idea but that if someone has any kind of problem or question, you're always there to listen. You should consider using a 'question box' for anonymous questions. If you have any suspicion at all that this may be an abuse situation, you should talk to the Child Protection member of staff.

Reproduction and birth (Part A)

KS2

In this lesson the children consider the major stages in someone's life. They see a video of human pregnancy and birth, and are told about sexual intercourse. They hear a story and then have the chance to ask questions anonymously.

Learning objectives for this lesson

Children will:

- know and understand about the processes of reproduction and birth as part of the human life cycle.

You will need

- Whiteboard/flip chart
- Video of human pregnancy and birth book: *Mummy Laid an Egg* by Babette Cole

Working agreement

Remind the children about the working agreement and emphasise the rule about treating each other with respect.

A

Opening activity

Time line of a human life: ask children to create a time line, which you put together on the board, of the life of a typical human being from birth to death. Include significant changes and developments, such as learning to walk, learning to talk, going to school, leaving school, getting a job, learning to drive, having children, and growing old. Talk about the life cycles of other animals, such as the frog, butterfly and dragonfly.

Main activities

You will probably want to use a video or other audio-visual aid to help with this. C4's *Living and Growing* programmes (Units 2 and 3) and the BBC's *Growing Up* are suitable and used in many schools across the country. Reference books for children will also help teachers find appropriate wording to describe sexual intercourse. Set the context by explaining that having sex is a way that adults express loving feelings for each other and is also the way a new baby is created or conceived. Explain as simply as you can the process of having sex, being pregnant and giving birth. A suggested explanation is given in the box below.

Explain briefly that if the couple do not want to have a baby they can use contraception, such as the pill or condoms or other methods.

Closing activity

Get children to write any questions they have as a result of this lesson on pieces of paper and put them anonymously into a box to be answered at the start of the next lesson. Read *Mummy Laid an Egg* by Babette Cole.

Additional resources

Storybooks:

- *Window* by Jeannie Baker
- *Happy Birth Day* by Robie H Harris
- *Where Did I Come From* by Peter Mayle
- *How Did I Begin?* by Mick Manning and Brita Granstrom
- *Let's Talk About Where Babies Come From* by Robie H Harris
- *Babies* by Susan Meredith
- *How Are Babies Made?* by Alastair Smith

Differentiation

Children in the class will be more or less ready to learn about sexual intercourse, depending on their maturity and backgrounds, so you need to be aware of the range of their prior knowledge and likely exposure to sexual situations, which could include TV soaps, soft porn videos or real situations. Use one of the assessment techniques listed in Section 3 to establish what children know and pitch the lesson accordingly.

Children needing more of a challenge: could write an explanation of how humans reproduce for a creature from another planet to read.

Children with additional learning needs: may need further opportunities to read and talk through one of the books listed above in a small group with a learning assistant.

Assessment

The questions which are put into the box at the end of the lesson should be a good indication of what the children have learned and what they are still not clear about.

What if...

...the questions in the box are silly or offensive?

Ignore them but be aware that they may reveal a fundamental lack of understanding that you may need to address or an inappropriate comment that may need to be challenged generally within an activity.

Brief example of a description of intercourse, conception, pregnancy and birth

Now that you know about all the parts of the body you can learn about the amazing way that babies are made and we will find out about sexual intercourse, conception, pregnancy and birth.

To make a baby you need sperm from a man's body to join with a tiny ovum (egg) from a woman's body. This is how it happens. When two adults get very fond of each other and care for each other they will really enjoy touching each other's bodies. They may decide that they want to have sex (or sexual intercourse) with each other, which is when the man puts his penis into the woman's vagina.

After touching and stroking each other and kissing each other, their bodies become very excited and this causes the man's penis to become stiff (called having an erection). The woman's vagina becomes wet and slippery and this makes it easy for the man to slide his penis into the vagina. The man and the woman move about and it feels very nice for them both and may make them both have an orgasm. For the woman, an orgasm gives her very nice feelings around her vagina and clitoris and all over her body. The man also feels very excited and semen comes out of his penis and into the woman's vagina. This is called ejaculation.

The sperm cells in the semen travel up into the woman's womb and on into the fallopian tubes where one of them might join up with (fertilise) an ovum from the ovaries. If they meet and join up, this is the very beginning of a baby. The fertilised ovum then travels back to the womb and settles into the womb lining and starts to grow. It will go on growing for about nine months – this is called pregnancy. When the baby is ready to be born, the muscles around the entrance to the womb will gradually work to stretch it open and push the baby out through the vagina, which also stretches so that the baby can get through, and the baby is born. Giving birth is hard work.

Reproduction and birth (Part B)

KS2

In this lesson the children discuss the help and care that babies need to grow and develop. They consider the skills and qualities that parents and carers need to look after babies and toddlers, and reflect on their own abilities to help with this.

Learning objectives for this lesson

Children will:

- understand what babies need in order to be happy and healthy
- understand the demands of looking after a baby
- think about how they can help care for babies and young children they know.

You will need

- Flip chart or whiteboard
- Pictures of babies and toddlers at different stages of development
- Baby care catalogues
- *Dr Xargle's Book of Earthlets* by Willis and Ross (optional)
- *Flour Babies* by Ann Fine (for additional activity)

Working agreement

Remind the children about the working agreement and emphasise the importance of respecting differences between individuals and families.

A

Opening activity

Show the class some pictures of newborn babies. Ask if any of them know any new babies among their family or friends. Ask them to think about what newborn babies are like, all the things they can and can't do and need help with, and how dependent they are on people to care for them. You could ask them to bring in some baby clothes to remind them just how small new babies are.

Alternatively, invite a parent and young baby to visit the class to talk about what the baby needs in terms of being looked after. Children could prepare questions prior to the visit. A health visitor might also be able to come in.

Main activities

Divide the class into groups to work on the following tasks.

- Create a timetable of all the things a parent or carer has to do in a day to look after a young baby.
- Using baby catalogues, work out how much it would cost to buy clothes and equipment for a new baby.

- Create a chart showing how babies grow and develop new skills, such as sitting up, crawling, feeding, walking, learning to use a potty, learning to talk, playing with more complex toys.
- Make a list of all the ways in which babies need to be kept physically safe and healthy (warmth, food, to be kept clean, secure environment with no dangers) and all the ways babies need to be helped to develop emotionally and intellectually (love, affection, play, reading, company, fun).

Ask the groups to report back to the whole class on what they have been doing. Lead them into a discussion of all the things parents and carers have to be able to do to bring up a baby to be healthy and safe. Record these ideas on a flip chart or whiteboard around a picture of a young baby and a toddler. Emphasise how much time it takes to look after a baby and how important it is for babies to be loved and played with as well as being clothed and fed.

Closing activity

You may want to read *Dr Xargle's Book of Earthlets* by Willis and Ross.

Go round the class asking children to say what they could do to help look after a baby or a toddler. Remind them that a baby always needs an adult around and that they should always ask an adult before doing anything with a baby.

Additional activity

Some teachers may like to get their class to look after an egg (hardboiled – or uncooked if you are brave enough) or a bag of flour as if it were a baby for a day or a week. Children can draw or paint a face and make a cradle and a shawl for their 'baby'. Just as if it were a real baby, it must not be left alone and must be treated very carefully at all times (so that it doesn't break or leak). After the set time, discuss how they felt about having this responsibility. *Flour Babies* by Anne Fine describes how a boy had to do this at school and the emotions he experiences.

Differentiation

Children needing more of a challenge: could design a mobile, pram rattle or a book for a baby or toddler.

Children with additional learning needs: could make a collage, using images from baby care catalogues showing all the things babies and toddlers need at different stages.

Assessment

Observe the children as they go about their activities and listen to what they say and reflect on whether there is a need for further work to develop their knowledge and thinking on this topic.

What if…

…someone says ‘When my baby brother cries my mum gets really cross’?

Use this as an opportunity to explain how difficult it can be when babies cry and cry especially in the middle of the night and that parents and carers can sometimes find it overwhelming and like any of us lose their temper. Explain that the baby isn’t doing it on purpose and that it can’t help crying. Say that a health visitor or a GP may be able to help suggest things that can help.

KS2

Growing and changing: Puberty

In this lesson children create their own personal time lines or draw themselves now and in the future. They see a video about changes at puberty and are given the opportunity to have separate gender, question-and-answer sessions. They also consider emotional changes.

Learning objectives for this lesson

Children will:

- know and understand about the physical changes that take place at puberty
- recognise and understand changing emotions as they grow up.

You will need

- Diagrams or pictures from a published scheme, magazines or the internet
- Paper for a time line
- Video, such as C4's *Living and Growing,* Units 2 and 3 or the BBC's *Growing Up: Sex education* and the associated teacher's pack and workbook
- Book: *Hair in Funny Places* by Babette Cole
- The *4You* booklet, *It's OK to Be You: Feeling good about growing up* and *Let's Talk about Sex* could be useful

Working agreement

Remind the children about the working agreement and emphasise the rule about treating each other with respect.

A

Opening activity

Time line to age 20: invite children to create their own personal time line, from birth to the present, with significant developments and changes. They should include, for example, learning to walk and to talk; going to nursery school; siblings being born; moving house; getting a new step family; starting school; learning to read, swim, and ride a bike. Leave space for a projected time line up to the age of about 20. Ask the children what they think will happen to them in that time (for example, move on to secondary school, pass exams, learn to drive, meet new friends). Sum up by saying that we all grow and change throughout our lives.

Alternatively, ask the children to draw a picture of themselves as they are now, and another of themselves as they think they might be when they are 20, and write the main changes that will have taken place. Get them to include physical changes as well as changed relationships, new skills and qualifications.

Main activities

You may wish to use a video or book to help with this lesson (see You will need).

Describe the main physical changes at puberty, for boys and girls, in the context of their bodies preparing for the time when they can become parents.

It can be useful to arrange separate question-and-answer sessions for boys and girls at this point, and perhaps for the school nurse or a male member of staff to assist you with the sessions. Make sure in each session that, while focusing on the needs of the gender group, children also understand the changes in the opposite sex. Girls in particular will be interested to see examples of sanitary pads and tampons, but you may also show them to boys.

Come back together as a whole class, explain that as you are growing and changing during puberty, your feelings and emotions change too. The *4You* booklet, *It's OK to Be You: Feeling good about growing up* and *Let's Talk about Sex* all have material on emotional development.

Closing activity

Read *Hair in Funny Places* by Babette Cole.

Alternatively, ask children to reflect on what they are looking forward to when they grow up.

Differentiation

As with the previous lesson, there will be a wide range of maturity within your class with some children already experiencing pubertal changes.

Children needing more of a challenge: could create their own booklets about changes in puberty.

Children with additional learning needs: could do further work in small groups to draw, on body outlines, the changes that happen to boys and girls at puberty.

Assessment

You may like to end the session with a quiz, possibly with the girls setting questions for the boys on the changes which happen to girls, and vice versa.

What if...

...children who either are not very physically developed or perhaps are quite developed are singled out for ridicule?

The class' working agreement is very important here and should have something to say about not making personal remarks.

Brief summary of changes at puberty

Boys and girls

Remind children that all children, boys or girls, reach puberty at different ages and that this is perfectly normal. Puberty is the body preparing to be able to reproduce and create a new baby. Not only will they experience physical changes but they may also experience new feelings and emotions. All these change can be scary or overwhelming but they are perfectly normal.

Boys and girls will both grow taller and gain weight.
Boys and girls grow hair under their arms and around their genitals.
Boys and girls sweat more.
Some boys and some girls get spots on their faces, chests and backs.
Boys and girls may begin to feel emotional and moody or feel very 'giggly' and excitable.

Boys

Voices become deeper.
Hair begins to grow on their upper lip and chin.
Testicles start to make sperm.
Boys may have erections and 'wet dreams'.
They may start having feelings of attraction towards other people.

Girls

Hips grow wider and their breasts start to grow larger.
Ovaries start to produce eggs (ova).
Menstruation begins.
They may start having feelings of attraction towards other people.

Menstruation

When a girl reaches puberty, her ovaries will produce an egg (ovum) every month. The egg travels from the ovary along the fallopian tube towards the womb. During her life, a woman will produce four or five hundred eggs most of which will not be fertilised and will pass out of the body. Every month the womb prepares to receive a fertilised egg by making a thick, soft, spongy lining. If the egg arrives in the womb unfertilised, the egg and the lining of the womb will pass out through the vagina. It looks like thick blood and is called a period. To soak up the womb lining as it passes out through the vagina, girls and women use either an absorbent towel which is worn in their pants or a tampon which is inserted into the vagina. Periods will happen every month until the woman is about 50, unless an egg is fertilised by a sperm from a man. When a girl starts her periods, it means that she could get pregnant. On average, the amount of blood leaving the body is about half a small cupful or two tablespoonfuls.

Similarities and differences

KS2

In this lesson the children think of ways in which people are similar and different to each other, then go on to examine how their own views and attitudes also differ. They think about ways to respect differences and what can happen if they are not respected.

Learning objectives for this lesson

Children will:

- be able to respect other people's viewpoints and beliefs
- be able to see things from other people's viewpoints
- have considered why being different can provoke bullying and why this is unacceptable
- be able to express opinions, for example about relationships and bullying.

You will need

- Statements on cards for values continuum
- Book: *The Sneetches* by Dr Seuss

Working agreement

Remind the children about the working agreement and emphasise the importance of treating each other with respect.

A

Opening activity

Ask children to work in pairs, preferably with someone they don't know so well, and find two things they have in common and two things that are different. Get them to give feedback to the rest of the class about what the similarities and differences are. Discuss what's good about being similar and what's good about being different. Emphasise that we are all unique and how we should all be proud of our particular differences. Discuss whether the characteristics they have chosen are things you can choose or whether they are givens. Examples could include hair colour and skin colour; football team and favourite food.

Main activities

Values continuum: start by explaining that we can also have different opinions and beliefs from each other. Explain the idea of a values continuum – a line which represents how strongly you agree with something from 'strongly agree' to 'strongly disagree'. You can do this as a physical activity, using an imaginary line across the classroom along which children stand according to their views about a series of statements (see examples of statements below). Alternatively, you can get children to work in groups using statements on cards and a line on a sheet of paper to indicate their views.

Statements

You will need to adapt these to reflect the interests of your class.

- Being a vegetarian is stupid.
- Children should give half their pocket money to charity.
- Teasing people and name-calling makes them unhappy.
- You shouldn't lend your things to a friend.
- You should always do what your parents or carers tell you to do.
- If you are in a hurry it is okay to run across the road/down the corridor.
- School holidays are boring.

Read the statements out and ask children to indicate whether they agree or disagree. Ask one child to explain their views, then ask for someone who has a different opinion to explain theirs. Compliment the class on how well they listened to each other.

Afterwards, discuss what it felt like when someone had a very different opinion from others. Ask them: Does it mean you are wrong? Explain that lots of people have lots of different ideas and we can disagree with their ideas without disliking them or being horrible to them. Ask: How can we show that we respect each other's views even if we disagree with them? (Answers are likely to include: listening, asking questions, politely saying you don't agree.)

Ask: What happens when people don't respect each other's views and don't respect others' differences? (Expect the answers: teasing, bullying, fighting, even wars.) Explain about discrimination and bullying being based on people not liking others being different and treating them differently.

Closing activity

Read *The Sneetches* by Dr Seuss.

Go round the class asking children to complete the sentence 'It's good to be friends with people who are different from you because...'.

Differentiation

Children needing more of a challenge: could hold a formal debate, with speakers on each side of the argument, and then take a vote at the end.

Children with additional learning needs: could work with puppets to make up small plays or sketches about what happens when people disagree with each other and how they can still get on with each other.

Assessment

Go round the class asking children to complete the sentences 'One thing I value about myself is...' and 'One thing I value about other people is...'.

What if…

…someone says something about another child or adult that is clearly offensive and is related to difference (such as skin colour, sexual orientation or size)?

You will need to challenge the comment using the working agreement and referring to the values of the school. You might want to ask the class: How would you feel if someone said something nasty about you because of a way that you're different to them?

Feelings

KS2

In this lesson the children identify a range of feelings and put names to them. They create examples of what different feelings can look like, then discuss how the body experiences different feelings. Finally, they think of ways in which we can make ourselves and others feel better when feeling 'down'. Teachers will find further ideas and resources for tackling this theme in the SEAL materials (DfES 2005).

Learning objectives for this lesson

Children will:

- recognise changing emotions in friends and family and be able to express their feelings positively
- be self-confident in a range of situations
- recognise their own worth and identify positive things about themselves
- be able to balance the stresses of life in order to promote both their own mental health and well-being and that of others.

You will need

- Paper or card and art materials

Working agreement

Remind the children about the working agreement to ensure a safe environment in which to share feelings. Emphasise that it is okay to show your feelings.

A

Opening activity

As a whole class or in groups, get the children to brainstorm all the 'feelings' words they can think of. Ask them to see if they can group them into categories. Create a class 'diary' of feelings, adding to it throughout the day and the week. You could create a 'feelings tree' on which children hang different coloured leaves to show how they are feeling at different times in the day or week.

Main activities

Frozen images: divide children into groups and get them to create a 'frozen image' relating to one of the categories of feelings words developed above. Other groups try to guess what feeling they are representing. Talk about how we know what someone is feeling – by their facial expression, the way they hold themselves. Then talk about how different feelings affect your body on the inside – butterflies in your tummy, heart beating faster, hot face, wobbly knees, feet made of stone, heart sinking, feel like flying. You could make a display to illustrate some of these.

Some feelings are positive and joyful, others can be more uncomfortable. In a circle, ask children to give an example of something that has given them a 'down' feeling, such as sadness, by completing the sentence 'I felt down when …'. Then ask them to come up with some suggestions about what someone can do to make themselves feel better when they are down about something. Then ask for suggestions about how they could help someone else who is feeling down. (Be sensitive to any child who may have a parent or carer with depression who they may be helping on a daily basis.)

Closing activity

Get children to make 'little books of calm', like the ones you see in bookshops, with six helpful suggestions about what you can do if you're feeling down. This could be done in a concertina-type book using a long strip of paper that is folded into different pages which then open out.

Additional activity

ICT: Children can use 'Google Image Search' to find pictures to illustrate a range of emotions. They can then create a simple card game matching picture to words.

Differentiation

Children needing more of a challenge: could create a 'feelings dictionary' using as many different words as possible for each feeling.

Children with additional learning needs: could make a small 'feelings book' with one word or phrase per page, for example 'This person feels sad because…', and a line drawing of a face.

Children could pair up with a 'feelings friend' who can note how they feel each day and talk to them about it.

Assessment

Note how the children's vocabulary or emotions are developing over the course of the week. Reflect on whether they need further work in this area, using poetry or fiction for example to learn new feelings words.

What if…

…the children do get better at expressing their feelings?

You may want to spend time talking about and exploring appropriate ways of expressing the negative ones such as anger. Some teachers have found that having a big floor cushion in another room that children can go and 'engage with' is a good idea. Also talk with them about what can happen if you bottle things up.

Keeping safe

KS2

In this lesson children identify what risky situations they might find themselves in, then go on to think about how they might behave in differing situations. There are links with the lesson 'Someone to talk to'.

Learning objectives for this lesson

Children will:

- know and understand about keeping themselves safe when involved with risky activities
- recognise the pressure of unwanted physical contact and know ways of resisting it
- understand when it is appropriate to take a risk and when to say no and seek help.

You will need

- Whiteboard or small cards (prepared)

Working agreement

Remind the children about the working agreement and emphasise that, although we should not talk about personal issues with the whole class, it is okay to speak to you or another teacher in private.

A

Opening activity

Note: You might first want to establish what the children think a risk is, since we do tend to think of them purely in terms of something negative. As a class or in small groups, brainstorm all the risky situations someone of their age might get involved in – at home, outside, at school and on the roads. Record children's responses on a whiteboard. Alternatively, make your own list of situations and write each one on a card. Divide the class in to small groups and give each group a card. Either as a whole class or in the small groups, ask them to put the situations in order of how risky they are. Talk about how activities can be risky but also exciting.

Main activity

Discuss each of the following situations in groups.

What are the risks and what would you do if:

- a friend's mum offers you a lift home from school
- a stranger asks you if you can show her the way to the shops
- your friends are all smoking and someone offers you one
- you are in a hurry to get home but the pedestrian crossing is red – there are no cars coming
- you find a saucepan boiling over on the cooker
- you find your mum's packet of pills on the coffee table

- an adult you don't know very well puts their arm around you
- at a friend's house, he/she suggests you try some of his/her parents' vodka
- you are scared of heights and your friend is trying to persuade you to climb to the top of a tree or climbing frame
- you see a group of children teasing another child.

Discuss answers as a whole class.

Closing activity

Based on the discussion of the situations above, make a list of useful strategies for keeping safe. Do this on the whiteboard or ask children to do this in their groups. The list could include: tell a grown-up, think before you act, say no, don't be pressured, remember road safety rules, always 'tell' if you are worried or scared or just feel that something is not right. You could then ask the children to illustrate them with a poster or PowerPoint presentation.

Additional activities

ICT: invite the children, in groups, to use a digital camera to create a 'freeze frame' of some of the risk scenarios. The children can then paste these into PowerPoint and label them with speech and thought bubbles and captions. Share these in assembly as well as in Key Stage 1 classes.

Differentiation

Children needing more of a challenge: could make a poster with simple safety rules for nursery and Key Stage 1 children.

Children with additional learning needs: could practise ways of saying *no* in different situations through role-play.

Assessment

Reflect on the list of strategies for keeping safe and consider whether the children need to do any further work in this area. Note if any children need additional support.

What if...

...you are asked or told by a pupil about something highly risky with which they, or another child (or even family member), is involved?

Don't dismiss what they have said but gently follow up on the working agreement by saying that this is something the child could talk to you about in private after the lesson. You would need to use your professional judgement as to what to do. If it involved suspicion of abuse or other kind of criminal activity, you would obviously report it to the headteacher and/or Child Protection Person and follow the school's Child Protection Procedures. Find a time to talk to them as soon as possible, do not promise confidentiality, and say you will try to get someone to help them. The teacher must provide consistent support during any referral or Child Protection Procedure.

Keeping yourself clean and healthy

KS2

In this lesson the children become familiar with a range of personal hygiene articles and products. They go on to discuss the importance of keeping clean and healthy. Finally, they learn about how infections can be prevented from passing from one person to another, looking in particular at HIV.

Learning objectives for this lesson

Children will:

- know and understand that you have to take extra care with personal hygiene during puberty
- know and understand that safe routines can stop the spread of viruses including HIV.

You will need

- Tray with objects relating to personal hygiene and something to cover them
- Two large body outlines for the group work and individual small ones for the closing activity
- Whiteboard or flip chart
- *Teaching and Learning about HIV: A resource for Key Stages 1 to 4* by Simon Blake and Paula Power (2003) could be useful

Working agreement

Remind the children about the working agreement and emphasise that we should not make personal remarks about others.

A

Opening activity

Play Kim's Game: use a range of objects and products relating to personal hygiene, such as soap, tissues, toothbrush or toothpaste, deodorant, sponge or flannel, towel, shampoo, nail brush, spot cream, razor, and clean socks or pants. Put the objects on a tray. Remove one object at a time (under a cloth so the children can't see) and get them to remember which object is missing. If you are doing this lesson in association with the lesson 'Growing and changing: puberty', you could include sanitary protection.

Discuss with the class why all these items are important as you get older and take more responsibility for looking after yourself. You could include other items such as hair gel, make-up, aftershave; then ask the children to divide all the items into essentials and non-essentials and get the children to decide which are the most important if they only had room in their bags for three of them.

Note: Your school nurse may be able to help you obtain free samples, for example of soap and toothpaste, for this lesson.

Main activity

Discuss with the class the two main reasons for keeping clean:

- so that we are pleasant to be with
- so that we keep healthy and don't either spread or catch germs and infections.

Use two body outlines, either on the whiteboard or flip chart, to record all the children's ideas about how infections pass from one person to another. (Expect answers like: sneezing, putting dirty hands in our mouths, infections in the air getting in when we cut ourselves, breathing in germs, touching someone.) Then discuss how we can protect ourselves as much as possible.

Talk with the class about a serious infection they may have heard of called HIV. Explain how it is not like other infections you have talked about today as it is transmitted (passed) from one person to another by getting from one person's bloodstream to another person's bloodstream or from one person's sexual organs to another's. It leads to a condition they may also have heard of called AIDS. In some countries, thousands of people have HIV and there is no cure. If a mother has HIV her baby may be born with it. To prevent it, all that people need to do is to avoid coming into close contact with someone else's blood and sexual parts. If the class already know about condoms, you can explain that they can be used to prevent passing on HIV. See the case study on page 96, taken from *Teaching and Learning about HIV: A resource for Key Stages 1 to 4* by Simon Blake and Paula Power (2003).

Closing activity

Get the class to make a list together of all the ways to keep clean and avoid infections as they grow up. You could do this using a body outline with labels and arrows.

Additional resources

Book: *Two Weeks with the Queen* by Morris Gleitzman. This novel, suitable for the 10–13 age group, tells the story of Colin who is sent from Australia to stay with relatives in England for a while because his brother has cancer. While in London, he decides to ask the Queen for help but in his search for her, he meets Ted and his partner Griff who are coping with AIDS. Despite the gloomy scenario the story is funny, wise and life-enhancing.

Differentiation

Children needing more of a challenge: could find out about how HIV affects children all over the world (see UNICEF and UNAIDS websites for more information).

Children with additional learning needs: could draw and label items to put in your suitcase when packing to go on holiday.

Assessment

Invite the children to come up with quiz questions (and answers) in small groups or teams. Then set up a quiz where they can use them on each other.

What if...

...there is a child being picked on by others because their personal hygiene is not what it should be?

You or the school nurse may choose to talk to the parent or carer about reasons for this happening and the resultant problems for the child. Remind the class of the working agreement about treating each other kindly. Maybe the school nurse, learning mentor or home school liaison worker could help.

CASE STUDY Focusing on HIV at Key Stage 2

This case study is from a primary school in South London and demonstrates how specific work on HIV is developed at Key Stage 2 (Blake and Power 2003).

The children are first asked what they already know about HIV using a class brainstorm.

Then an outline is drawn of two people on the board and, next to the relevant body parts, all the illnesses and infections that children can think of are written. The children are then asked to think about all the ways that illnesses can be passed between two people: for example through breathing, sneezing, hands/touching, getting very close to someone, kissing, sharing things you put in your mouth, sharing needles and through sex. It is explained that different illnesses are passed on in different ways. If they don't mention it you can then explain that sexual activity is another way that some infections can be passed on as people's bodies are in very close contact with each other and semen and vaginal fluids are passed from one person to another if they do not use a condom.

It is explained that there are a number of specific infections that can be spread through sex and one of these is HIV. It is explained that HIV is a virus and is a chronic health condition, which may lead to a whole number of HIV-related illnesses.

- The children are helped to remember how our immune system works – when infections get into the body, white blood cells rush around the body and fight it off.
- It is then explained that HIV is an especially nasty virus because the part of the body it attacks is the immune system, the bit in the body that is supposed to fight it off. When HIV gets in and attacks the immune system it means that all sorts of other germs, bacteria and viruses can move around the body without any way of being killed off.
- How people become infected with HIV is then addressed, emphasising that it is a difficult virus to transmit and lots of the ways that other viruses spread don't work for HIV. Go back to your people diagram and cross out the ways in which HIV *cannot* be transmitted (getting close; sitting next to; sharing cups, spoons, etc.; kissing; holding hands; via toilet seats; touching; sneezing) and stress that HIV can only be passed to another person through blood-to-blood transmission, sexual activity and breastfeeding.
- What happens if a person gets HIV is then explored, the symptoms and the treatments available.
- Emotions and responses to HIV are explored, by asking for example: What do you think someone who had just found out that they had HIV would feel like? What would they need? How would they want to be treated? Why are some people so scared about HIV and prejudiced towards people living with HIV? Why might some people not want to help someone who has HIV?

Someone to talk to

KS2

In this lesson the children explore why it can be difficult to ask for help. They identify sources of help in and out of school and then look at how we can help each other. They practise good listening. Speaking and listening is now a priority in literacy and this lesson can contribute to this.

Learning objectives for this lesson

Children will:

- be able to listen to and support others
- be able to identify adults they can trust and who they can ask for help
- be able to listen to and support their friends
- know where individuals, families and groups can get help.

You will need

- Whiteboard
- Card or paper

Working agreement

Remind the children about the working agreement and emphasise the importance of listening to each other.

A

Opening activity

In a circle, ask children to come up with answers to the question: Why is it important to have someone to talk to about problems? Follow this up with a discussion about why it might sometimes be difficult to tell someone your problems.

Main activities

Activity 1 Talk about all the different kinds of people you can go to if you need help – friends, family members, professionals (school nurse, GP, social worker), those manning helplines, as well as those accessible via the internet.

Get children to create their own personal directory of people they could talk to if they were worried about something, with phone numbers, email and web addresses, or where they can be found. For example:

Mum at work	0923 740937
Nan (Mrs XXX)	48239–58
School nurse (name)	in the medical room on Tuesdays
Learning mentor	in the staffroom on XXXX
ChildLine	0800 1111
Best friend	0922 928474

They could make this into a little card or booklet that they could keep in their school bag. (If you have laminating facilities in school, it might be possible to make the booklets more durable.)

Activity 2 Talk about how we can help each other – you may have a peer-mentoring or buddy scheme at the school so be sure to mention this. Divide children into groups and give each group one of the following scenarios.

What would you say or do if:

- your friend said he/she was being bullied?
- your friend said he is sad because his dad has gone away?
- your friend said he/she was feeling very worried about going on to secondary school?
- your friend said she is sad because her budgie has died?
- your friend says his big brother has broken his new PlayStation?

Then get the children to think about: how to talk to someone who confides in them, how they might be feeling, how you can be a good listener. Together, come up with a list of qualities of a good supportive listener.

Closing activity

Listening activity: Invite the children to form pairs. Tell one half of each pair (A) that they will be asked to talk about a pretend problem for a minute. Tell the other half of each pair (B), in private, that their partner will talk about a pretend problem for a minute and, for the first 30 seconds they (B) should use looks, smiles and nods to show they are concentrating on listening; then, at a signal, for the next 30 seconds use looking away, fidgeting, frowning, and the repeating of a daft phrase(s) to show they are not paying full attention.

Then ask the children to swap roles, explain what they now have to do and repeat the activity. Discuss how the different behaviours made them feel.

Go round the class asking children to complete the sentences 'It's good to be a good listener because…'.

Differentiation

Children needing more of a challenge: could make up their own problems; develop this into a newsletter of the examples children feel are the most common. Teacher to edit this, then deliver it to all Key Stage 2 classrooms.

Children with additional learning needs: could make a 'Time to listen' board. Each child or pair write something in a bubble for the board, such as: *Don't butt in! Be kind. Smile! Remember your body language. Suggest others who may be able to help.*

Assessment

Ask the children to be agony aunts and uncles and to write answers, either in small groups or individually, to problems that 'other children' (that is, you the teacher) have sent in. Ask the whole class whether they think the answers have contained good advice.

What if...

...a child should become upset and tearful in the lesson when they are talking about things that have made them sad?

You may want to take them out and get someone (administrative staff, Learning Support Assistant) to be with them until you can attend to them after the lesson. Alternatively, you may decide it can be handled in the classroom if you judge that the situation behind the behaviour may not be serious enough to warrant further exploration. You may decide, in fact, that it could be handled very well by the friends of the child concerned.

Friends

KS2

In this lesson the class looks at what makes a good friendship, how friendships sometimes go wrong and how friends can make up. Bullying and what to do about it is also included.

Learning objectives for this lesson

Children will:

- be able to express opinions, for example about relationships and bullying
- be self-confident in a wide range of situations, such as seeking new friends
- manage friendship problems
- understand about different forms of bullying and the feelings of both bullies and victims.

You will need

- Two puppets
- Whiteboard or flip chart

Working agreement

Remind the children about the working agreement for PSHE and Citizenship. Emphasise the rule about being kind to each other.

A

Opening activity

Brainstorm answers to the question: What are friends for? Then discuss the qualities we look for in a good friend – you could use a body outline on the board (write good friend on his or her chest) and record the children's answers round the outside.

Main activities

Discuss what goes wrong with friendships sometimes. Use two puppets to act out some of the scenarios the children have come up with. Get the children to think about how each puppet might be feeling, then to come up with some advice for the puppets about how they can make up.

Scenarios

- Natasha is upset because her best friend has made a new friend at the After School Club.
- Mark joins in with others teasing his friend David because his brother has Down's syndrome.
- Kelly's friend won't let her play with them because they say she's a swot/boff.
- A group of boys won't let Alex play football with them and are calling him gay.

Alternatively, get children to work in small groups or pairs to create 'frozen images' of friends who have fallen out, also include some bullying situations. Ask the rest of the class to interpret the image and think about how each person will be feeling and what they will be thinking. Then ask the children to create a new frozen image to show that the friends have made up and to explain how they did it.

Devise some questions that might be sent to an agony aunt about friendship and bullying issues and get the children to answer them in pairs. Then ask them, in turn, to give feedback to the whole class.

Closing activity

Go round the class asking children to complete the sentences:

- It's good to have friends because...
- A friend is someone who...
- I think bullying is wrong because...
- We can all try to stop bullying by...

Additional activities

ICT: invite the children, in groups, to use a digital camera to create freeze frame scenarios. The children can paste them into PowerPoint and label them with speech and thought bubbles and captions.

Differentiation

Children needing more of a challenge: could make digital pictures into a storyboard, with speech bubbles and captions, to be presented as a PowerPoint presentation.

Children with additional learning needs: could devise a story from digital pictures which could be videoed and played back to the class.

Assessment

You will get some sense of whether the children are taking these issues on board by your sense of how the atmosphere or ethos of your classroom changes over time, for example whether it seems calmer, whether children are talking more about feelings and how to solve problems. There may also be fewer issues in the playground over time or fewer instances recorded in the school bullying incident book.

What if...

...you are aware that a child in your class is the ringleader of a gang who may be intimidating and bullying other children in school?

Talk to the child about your concerns. Hear what they have to say: it may be that the bullying is the result of some unhappiness in their life. Remember that some children who bully may been bullied themselves. Involve other staff and parents if necessary. Check that your school anti-bullying policy has been reviewed recently. Follow the school's anti-bullying guidance and procedures.

Families of all kinds

KS2

In this lesson children identify the people who are closest to them – and they therefore see how these are different for different people. They discuss how we can show people that we care for them and also what to do if we quarrel sometimes. They learn that when someone goes away or dies, it can be very painful but that it can also be coped with.

Learning objectives for this lesson

Children will:

- be able to recognise their changing emotions towards their families
- be able to see things from other people's viewpoints, for example their parents' and carers'
- know and understand about the many relationships in which they are all involved
- have considered the need for trust and love in established relationships
- know and understand about, and accept, a wide range of different and diverse family arrangements, for example, married, divorced or separated parents, second marriages, fostering, extended families, same sex parents, and three or more generations living together
- have considered how separation and loss affect people in the family.

Note: The learning objectives cover sufficient ground to allow for an extension lesson, particularly for the fifth and sixth objectives.

You will need

- Medium or large sheets of paper
- Pens and pencils
- Whiteboard or flip chart

Working agreement

Remind the children about the working agreement and emphasise the rule about treating each other with respect.

A

Opening activity

Ask the children to think about all the people in their network of family, carers and friends. Ask them to draw a large circle on a sheet of paper with a small picture of themselves in the middle. Then ask them to draw pictures of all the people that are important to them, putting the most important closest to them and the rest at relative distances away. Emphasise that you are not talking about the physical distance that people live but emotional importance.

Make a list on a whiteboard or flip chart of all the different types of people they have included: parents, grandparents, foster parents, step-parents, aunts and uncles, cousins, friends, parents' friends and so on. Talk about how we all come from different family situations. Remind them of the work you have done on similarities and differences and how we should be proud and glad that we are all different and respect people's right to be different.

Main activities

Talk about what the people in our network do for us and what we do for them and how we can show we love them. You can invite children to illustrate this with drawings and captions, which you can then make into a class book or wall display.

Introduce the idea that we sometimes argue with the people we love and do things that hurt them. Use scenarios to talk about how we resolve arguments and get help if things get really bad. Here are some example scenarios.

- John's mum is really mad with him because his room is untidy.
- Erin and her brother are always fighting about whose turn it is to go on the PlayStation.
- Natasha's step-dad shouts at her because she's making too much noise when he's trying to watch TV.
- Darshan's mum has a big argument with her boyfriend and then bursts into tears.
- Darren's foster father won't let him play football after dark.
- Kelly's nan won't let her stay up to watch *Big Brother*.

You can also talk about what happens when someone you love goes away or dies, how it makes people feel and how we can help people cope with loss. Stress that it is okay to feel very sad and maybe angry when you 'lose' someone, but that talking to someone you trust can help and that eventually you will begin to feel better. Talk about what you can do if someone you know is feeling sad.

Closing activity

Go round the class asking children to complete the sentence: 'When I quarrel with someone in my family network, it helps if…' or 'We can show our special people we care about them by…'.

Additional activities

Silent statements: Ask the children to form a circle then explain that when you call out a statement, they need to check whether it applies to them. If it does, they will need to stand up and change places with someone else without speaking. In this version, you could call out one of the following variations: 'All those who have their mum/gran/step-dad/older sister/stepsister/cousin/friends/carer living with them/in their family/in their network…' stand up and change places. Again, stress how many different people the children are close to.

This could be a good opportunity to discuss issues around same sex parents and sexual orientation. Give a simple explanation of what it means and say that some people prefer to have close relationships with someone of the same sex. For example, in the same way as men and women can be attracted and love each other so too can two men or two women.

Differentiation

Children needing more of a challenge: could write a short play based on one of the scenarios discussed.

Children with additional learning needs: could use a digital camera and create a storyboard on one of the scenarios.

Additional resources

Storybooks:

- *Flour Babies* by Anne Fine
- *Goggle Eyes* by Anne Fine
- *Dogger* by Shirley Hughes
- *Badger's Parting Gifts* by S Varley
- *My Dad Takes Care of Me* by Patricia Quinlan and Vlasta Van Kampen
- *At Daddy's on Saturdays* by Linda Walvoord Girard
- *Asha's Mums* by Rosamund Elwin and Michele Paulse

Assessment

Listen and observe the children throughout all the activities and use your reflections to plan further lessons based on their needs.

What if...

...there is a child in the class who has two mothers? (She calls both of them *Mum*, but you overhear a child saying 'But you can't have two mums...')

It may not be appropriate to speak to the child unless you know that they are being hassled about it, but you do need to make the class aware that single-sex partnerships are very much part of the range of family types. You may choose to talk to her mum and partner to see how they want to handle things. There is a good book called *Asha's Mums* by Rosamund Elwin and Michele Paulse which, although aimed more at Key Stage 1 children, may be something you'd like to read with the class.

Choices and consequences

KS2

In this lesson the children consider a range of scenarios and look at the consequences of possible actions.

Learning objectives for this lesson

Children will:

- be able to form opinions which they can articulate to a variety of audiences
- be able to discuss moral questions
- know and understand that their actions have consequences and be able to anticipate the results of them
- understand and be able to resist peer and media pressure.

You will need

- Small prepared cards for opening activity (if using desk version)
- Scenarios for main activity written on cards or a whiteboard

Working agreement

Remind the children about the working agreement and emphasise the importance of listening to each other.

A

Opening activities

Values continuum: Use the following statements for a values continuum across the room or on paper. Alternatively, put them on cards and ask the children to work in small groups to place each card on pieces of paper marked agree/disagree.

Statements

- It's worse to hit someone than to say unkind things to them.
- If your friend tells you about a problem and asks you to keep it secret, it's wrong to tell anyone else about it.
- It's okay to take 50p from your mum's purse without asking.
- You should own up if someone gets told off when you know it's your fault.
- It's okay to say nasty things about a person as long as they don't know you're doing it.

Hear their answers and make sure everyone is aware that there are differing views. Explain the concept of peer and media pressure.

Main activities

Below are a number of scenarios. Use them as a basis for the children to discuss the choices made by the protagonists. You could either organise the children into small groups and give each group a scenario to discuss before asking them to give feedback to the whole class; or you could use the scenarios as a basis for role-plays.

Scenarios

- Kirsten is with a group of friends. They are trying to persuade her to go with them to try a bit of shoplifting. What will be the consequences if she says no and goes home – how would she feel? What will be the consequences if she goes with them – how would she feel and what might happen?
- Amal sees another boy being teased by a group of children because he isn't wearing the latest trainers. He can either pass by without doing anything or he can go back to school and tell a teacher. What would be the consequences of each action? How might he be feeling and what should he do?
- Mary's friends are trying to persuade her to bully a girl in their class. She can either do what they want or turn her back and go and play with someone else? What would be the consequences of each action? How might Mary be feeling?
- Tom's mum always makes him a packed lunch with brown-bread sandwiches, salad, fruit and water. He wants to have chocolate bars, crisps and fizzy drinks like some of his friends. He can either eat the lunch his mother gives him or throw it away and have no lunch. What are the consequences of each action?
- Daisy's mum won't let her read teenage magazines like her friends because she thinks they aren't suitable for a girl of her age (10). She can either do what her mum says or secretly read her friends' magazines. Why does Daisy's mum not want her to read the magazines? Why does Daisy want to read them? What should Daisy do? What would be the consequences of each action?

After hearing feedback on each scenario, ask the class: What would *you* do? How are the best decisions made?

Closing activity

Go round the class asking children to complete the sentence: 'When I'm trying to decide what to do and how to act, it helps if I ...'.

Differentiation

The lesson is discussion-based so you need to consider ways to involve those children who are either naturally rather quiet in groups or whose English is not fluent. Drawing cartoons and making storyboards of a decision-making scenario could help. These could then be displayed and act as a record of the lesson.

Children needing more of a challenge: could take one of the scenarios and make a decision flow chart showing what would happen if different decisions were made.

Children with additional learning needs: could take one of the scenarios and role-play the consequences of different decisions.

Assessment

Observe the feedback from the scenarios closely and reflect on how the children reacted and the reasons they gave for particular actions. Decide whether they need further work on moral issues and decision making.

What if...

...a child consistently suggests inappropriate behaviours such as stealing or cheating?

Make sure that you allow plenty of opportunities for children to question each other and always ask the class to reflect on what the consequences would be both for themselves and others. You may wish to explore using the Philosophy for Children approach to thinking about choices (for further details of Philosophy for Children see www.teachingthinking.net/thinking/pages/robert_fisher_webresources.htm). Many Citizenship resources will include ideas for exploring moral dilemmas.

Gender and sexuality

KS2

In this lesson the children look at the differences between the sexes by focusing on how our society treats them both. They consider gender roles and stereotyping.

Learning objectives for this lesson

Children will:

- be able to recognise and challenge gender stereotypes
- have considered why being different can provoke bullying and why this is unacceptable
- understand how the media impact on forming attitudes.

You will need

- Picture, model or toy of an alien
- Picture of a baby
- Magazine pictures of people
- Birthday cards, new baby cards and magazine pictures showing gender stereotyping

Working agreement

Remind the children about the working agreement and emphasise the importance of treating each other with respect.

A

Opening activity

Introduce a picture, model or soft toy representation of an alien (you can even get inflatable ones) explaining to the class that this creature comes from a planet where they don't have male and female, so that he doesn't know how to tell the difference between girls and boys. Ask the class to tell him what the differences are. Record their answers.

Main activity

Find a picture of a baby (try to find one that is fairly non-gender specific – so no blue or pink clothes!). Divide the class into two groups and tell one group that the baby is a girl and the other that it is a boy. Ask the children to draw and write about how they think the baby will grow up at ages 5, 11, 16 and 25 – its physical and emotional characteristics, toys it will play with, games it will play, clothes it will be wearing, hobbies it will have, jobs it might be doing and so on.

Then reveal that they were both looking at the same person and talk about the difference that being a boy or a girl makes in a person's life. Discuss whether there is only one way of behaving if you are a boy or a girl.

Alternatively, show pictures of a variety of adults, male and female and of different backgrounds. With children working individually at first, invite them to write on the back of the picture the occupation that they think that adult might have. Then get the children to share their ideas in groups, each child explaining the reason they chose that occupation for that particular adult.

Be ready to challenge some of the assumptions by giving examples of non-stereotypical working roles: a man staying at home to look after children, a woman bus driver, a male nurse, a female firefighter, and so on.

Discuss where we get our ideas about gender roles. Collect images from magazines, birthday cards and new baby cards and discuss how men and women are portrayed. Introduce and explain the word *stereotype*. What would happen if a boy or a girl wanted to do something that didn't fall within the stereotyped role? (Children may have seen the films *Billy Elliott, Bend it like Beckham*.) What would family and friends say? How might the boy or girl feel? Talk about teasing and bullying because someone is different.

This could be a good opportunity to discuss issues around sexual orientation, especially if terms like 'gay' are used if boys or girls do not comply with gender stereotypes. Give a simple explanation of what being 'gay' means and say why it is unacceptable to use it as an insult (refer back to the feelings lesson), for example, in the same way as men and women can be attracted to and love each other so can two men or two women.

Closing activity

Go round the class asking children to complete the sentence 'Something that we've talked about today that has made me think is…'.

Additional resources

- Book: *Bill's New Frock* by Anne Fine
- Book: *The Paper Bag Princess* by Robert N Munsch
- Video and teacher's pack: C4's *Living and Growing*, Girl Talk Boy Talk (it covers the subject of media pressure well)

Invite visitors who challenge stereotypes to discuss their jobs, for example a male nurse, female firefighter.

Differentiation

Children needing more of a challenge: could write a story in which traditional gender roles are reversed.

Children with additional learning needs: could design a birthday or new baby card that would be suitable for both sexes.

Assessment

You will get a sense of children's attitudes and ideas from their discussion and can therefore decide whether to do more work on this area in the future.

What if…

…someone says 'My dad says that women should stay at home and look after the house'?

Open it up for class discussion. Ask: What do you think mums should do? Can dads stay at home and look after the house? Make sure that it is emphasised that everyone has the right to make their own decisions and that we all have the right to our own ideas.

6 Resources and contacts

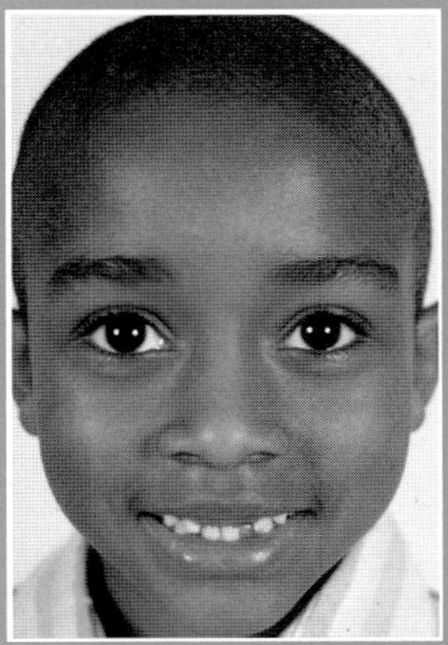

6 Resources and contacts

Resources

For up-to-date lists of available resources, for primary, secondary and special schools, visit Sex Education Forum's website www.ncb.org.uk/sef

Storybooks, fiction and non-fiction

Baker, J (2002) *Window*. Walker ISBN: 0744594863

Cole, B (1995) *Mummy Laid an Egg*. Red Fox. ISBN: 0099299119

Cole, B (2001) *Hair in Funny Places*. Red Fox. ISBN: 0099266261

Elwin, R and Paulse, M (1990) *Asha's Mums*. Women's Press of Canada. ISBN: 0889611432

Fine, A (1994) *Flour Babies*. Puffin. ISBN: 0140361472

Fine, A (2002) *Bill's New Frock*. Egmont Books. ISBN: 140520060X

Fine, A and Aldous, K (2004) *Goggle Eyes*. Puffin. ISBN: 0140340718

Garland, S (1993) *Billy and Belle*. Puffin. ISBN: 0140544372 Out of print

Girard, L Walvoord (1991) *At Daddy's on Saturdays*. Albert Whitman. ISBN: 0807504734

Gleitzman, M (2003) *Two Weeks with the Queen*. Puffin. ISBN: 0141314559

Harris, RH (1998) *Happy Birth Day.* Walker. ISBN: 0744552648

Harris, RH (2004) *Let's Talk About Where Babies Come From.* Walker. ISBN: 1844281736

Hiawyn, O and Kitamuri, S (2004) *Angry Arthur*. Red Fox Picture Books. ISBN: 0099196611

Hughes, S (1993) *Dogger*. Red Fox Picture Books. ISBN: 009992790X

Manning, M and Granstrom, B (1999) *My Body Your Body*. Franklin Watts. ISBN: 0749658622

Manning, M and Granstrom, B (2004) *How Did I Begin?* Franklin Watts. ISBN: 0749656611

Mayle, P (1993) *Where Did I Come From.* Pan. ISBN: 0330331132

Meredith, S (2005) *Babies.* Usborne. ISBN: 0746031548

McKee, D (1982) *Not Now Bernard*. Red Fox. ISBN: 0099240505

McKee, D (1999) *Elmer the Story of a Patchwork Elephant*. Red Fox. ISBN: 0099400049 Out of Print

Munsch, RN and Martchenko, M (1999) *The Paper Bag Princess*. Little Hippo. ISBN: 0439010179

Murphy, J (2003) *A Piece of Cake.* Walker Books. ISBN: 0744557712

Quinlan, P and Van Kampen, V (2000) *My Dad Takes Care of Me*. Annick Press. ISBN 092030379X

Seuss, Dr (2003) *The Sneetches.* Collins. ISBN: 0007158505

Smith, A (2000) *How Are Babies Made?* Usborne. ISBN: 0746025025

Varley, S (1992) *Badger's Parting Gifts*. Picture Lions. ISBN: 0006643175 Reprinting

Willis, J and Ross, T (2001) *Dr Xargle's Book of Earthlets*. Andersen Press. ISBN: 1842700677

Non-fiction for children

fpa (2003) *4You – Growing Up: What's it all about?* Booklet.

fpa (1994) *Periods: What you need to know*. Booklet.

Harris, Robie and Emberley, Michael (2005) *Let's Talk About Sex: A book about changing bodies, growing up, sex and sexual health*. Walker Books. ISBN: 1844281744

Patterson, Claire and Quilter, Lindsay (1991) *It's OK to be You: Feeling good about growing up.* Piccolo Books. ISBN: 0330313630 Out of print

Teaching packs and videos

Living and Growing, Channel 4. Units 1, 2 and 3; 15 minutes each. Also teacher's book and other SRE materials for primary schools

Contact details

Email: 4learning.sales@channel4.co.uk

Tel: 08701 246 444

Fax: 08701 246 446

Post: 4Learning, PO Box 400, Wetherby, LS23 7LG

http://www.4learningshop.co.uk/ShowProductsFromSearch.cfm

Birth, Care and Growth. BBC three programmes for 5–7 year olds, 15 minutes each. Distributed by BBC Education Publishing, Tel: 0870 100200

Growing up: Sex Education. three programmes for 9–11 year olds, 15 minutes each. Distributed by BBC Education Publishing. Tel: 0870 100200

Contact details

www.bbcschoolshop.com/

Some of Your Bits Ain't Nice. Personal hygiene video, 10 minutes (1994) Health Education Council/Health Education Authority

Contact details

Health promotion/education libraries may still have copies; also available from Concord Video and Film Council, Ipswich, to buy for £25 plus p & p and VAT, or on free loan for up to 14 days. Tel: 01473 726012

Making Sense of Growing Up and Keeping Safe. An interactive CD-Rom for primary schools aimed at Key Stage Two. Published by National Children's Bureau and Sense Interactive CDs.

All About Life. Lesley de Meza and Stephen De Silva, Forbes Publications (2004) ISBN: 1899527222

The Baby's Catalogue. Allan and Janet Ahlberg. Puffin (1984) 0140503854

Blake, S and Muttock, S (2004) *Assessment, Evaluation and Sex and Relationships Education*. London: National Children's Bureau

Job, Nina and Frances, Gill (2004) *Childhood Bereavement: Developing the curriculum and pastoral support*. National Children's Bureau/Childhood Bereavement Network. ISBN: 1904787142

Blake, Simon and Power, Paula (2003) *Teaching and Learning about HIV: A resource for Key Stages 1 to 4*. Sex Education Forum/National Children's Bureau. ISBN: 1904787088 (available to download from www.ncb.org.uk/sef)

Websites – for pupils and teachers

For Key Stage 1 pupils

www.welltown.gov.uk/
www.childline.org.uk

For Key Stage 2 pupils

www.healthfreak.org.uk
www.galaxy-h.gov.uk/
www.dr-ann.org
www.missdorothy.com
www.unicef.org.uk (with adult supervision)

For teachers

www.unicef.org.uk (This site has a special 'Teacherzone' page.)
www.savethechildren.org
www.kidscape.org.uk
www.wiredforhealth.gov.uk/
www.teachernet.gov.uk/teachingandlearning/
www.bbc.co.uk/schools/
www.channel4.com/learning/
www.circle-time.co.uk
For more information on teaching resources and lesson plans see the Teachernet website (www.teachernet.gov.uk/teachingandlearning/).
Sex Education Forum/National Children's Bureau Resources
NCB Booksales details:
www.ncb-books.org.uk
0207 843 6029
sales@ncb-books.org.uk

References

Blake, S and Muttock, S (2004) *Assessment, Evaluation and Sex and Relationships Education*. London: National Children's Bureau.

Department for Education and Employment (2000) *Sex and Relationship Education Guidance*. London: Department for Education and Employment. (0116/2000)

Department for Education and Skills (2004a) *PSHE in Practice: Resource pack for teachers in primary schools*. London: Department for Education and Skills.

Department for Education and Skills (2004b) *Safeguarding Children in Education*. London: Department for Education and Skills.

Department for Education and Skills (2004c) *Every Child Matters: Change for children in schools.* London: Department for Education and Skills.

Department for Education and Skills (2005) *Excellence and Enjoyment: Social and emotional aspects of learning* (SEAL) London: Department for Education and Skills.

Department for Education and Skills and Home Office (2004) *PSHE in Practice: Primary pack.* London: Department for Education and Skills.

Department of Health (2003) *What to do if you're worried a child is being abused*. London: Department of Health.

Department of Health (2005) *National Healthy School Status: A guide for schools*. London: Department of Health.

Education Act 1996. Chapter 56. London: HMSO.

fpa/Mori 'Sex Education Lessons for Parents from fpa', *MORI* (2000). www.mori.com/polls/2000/fpa.shtml (accessed 20 March 2005).

Frances, G and Power, P (2003) *Developing Sex and Relationships Education in Schools: Guidance and training activities pack for school governors*. London: National Children's Bureau.

Goleman, DP (1995) *Emotional Intelligence: Why it can matter more than IQ for character, health and lifelong achievement*. London: Bantam Books.

Ingham, R and van Zessen, G (1998) *From Cultural Contexts to Interactional Competencies: A European comparative study,* an invited paper presented at *AIDS in Europe: Social and Behavioural Dimensions,* Paris 12–16 January 1998.

Margetts, D and Lynch, M (2004) 'Fun without fear', *Spotlight,* 4, Nov. 2004

Martinez, A (2005) *Effective Learning Methods: Approaches to teaching about Sex and relationships within PSHE and Citizenship.* London: National Children's Bureau.

Office for Standards in Education (2002) *Sex and Relationships: A report from Her Majesty's Chief Inspector of Schools* (HMI 433). London: Office for Standards in Education.

Qualifications and Curriculum Authority (1999a) *The National Curriculum Handbook for Primary Teachers in England*. London: Qualifications and Curriculum Authority.

Qualifications and Curriculum Authority (1999b) *The Standards Site: Science at Key Stages 1 and 2,* http://www.standards.dfes.gov.uk/schemes2/science/?view=get

Sex Education Forum (2002) *Faith, Values and Sex and Relationships Education*. London: Sex Education Forum.

Sex Education Forum (2004) *Faith, Values and Sex and Relationships Education*. Forum Factsheet, London: National Children's Bureau.

Sex Education Forum (2005) *Sex and Relationships Education Framework*. London: Sex Education Forum.

Sex Education Forum (2006) *Call for PSHE, which includes sex and relationships education, to be made statutory*. London: National Children's Bureau.

Social Exclusion Unit (1999) *Teenage Pregnancy*. London: Stationery Office. (Cm 4342).

The National Society (2002) *Educating Children and Young People in School about Marriage*. London: Church House Publishing.

Appendix 1: Sample letter to parents of Key Stage 1 or Key Stage 2 children

Below is a sample of a letter you can send to parents of Key Stage 1 or 2 to accompany an overview of the lessons in this pack and ideas for their involvement, for example a book to read at home.

Dear ....,

I am writing to let you know that, over the next [*insert number*] of weeks, starting next [*insert date*], your child's class will be taking part in some Personal, Social and Health Education lessons which will include Sex and Relationships Education.

This is part of the whole-school Personal, Social & Health Education programme which is taught right through the school in every year and which is monitored and reviewed regularly by the staff and governing body.

Topics being taught to your child's class are:

- Male and female/body parts
- Growing and changing
- Similarities and differences
- Feelings
- Keeping Safe
- Keeping yourself clean and healthy
- Someone to talk to
- Friends
- Families of all kinds
- Choices and consequences
- Gender stereotypes/Gender and sexuality

You will have an opportunity to see the materials being used in the lessons including books and videos next ....[*insert time/date*]

If this date does not suit you, please contact your child's class teacher who will make arrangements to talk to you about the lessons.

Yours sincerely,

[*Headteacher*]